INTERACTIVE WEB APPLICATION DEVELOPMENT ANGULAR AND TYPESCRIPT

DR. AMOL PRAKASH BHAGAT | FAIZAN SHAH | KIRAN N. KHAKARE | BHASKAR R. HARLE | AND KALIDAS S. BHAWALE

Made with ♥ on the Notion Press Platform
www.notionpress.com

To those who dare to click, code, and create—an ode to the dreamers, the problem-solvers, and the relentless pursuers of seamless interactivity. May your lines of code be bug-free and your user experiences be truly engaging. This book is dedicated to the builders of the web, shaping the digital landscapes of tomorrow with every keystroke and commitment to the craft.

To the Angular architects and JavaScript enthusiasts, whose passion for elegant code and dynamic web applications knows no bounds. This book is dedicated to the trailblazers who navigate the complex terrain of Angular with unwavering dedication. May your directives be clear, your dependencies minimal, and your applications truly shine. Here's to the developers who turn challenges into opportunities and transform ideas into interactive realities.

To the TypeScript trailblazers, who navigate the realms of static typing with grace and wield the power of clarity in every line of code. This book is dedicated to the architects of robust and scalable applications, where types dance in harmony, and errors reveal themselves willingly. May your interfaces be impeccable, your transpilations seamless, and your journeys through the typed landscape be both enlightening and rewarding. Cheers to the developers who embrace the future with every keystroke and declaration.

Contents

Foreword

In the ever-evolving landscape of the digital realm, interactivity has become the heartbeat of the web. As we navigate through a sea of pixels and possibilities, the ability to engage users seamlessly has become a hallmark of exceptional web development.

In this meticulously crafted guide to interactive web application development, the authors take us on a journey through the intricacies of creating immersive and responsive user experiences. With each chapter, they unveil the secrets behind crafting dynamic interfaces, handling asynchronous interactions, and breathing life into static pages.

More than just a manual, this book is a companion for the developers who dare to dream beyond static screens. It is a roadmap for those who seek to master the art of creating applications that not only function flawlessly but also captivate and delight users.

From the fundamentals to advanced techniques, the authors leave no stone unturned, offering insights, best practices, and real-world examples that empower developers to elevate their skills. Whether you're a seasoned coder or a newcomer to the world of web development, this book is a valuable resource that demystifies the complexities of building interactive applications.

As we embark on this journey through the pages that follow, may you find inspiration, guidance, and a renewed passion for the craft of interactive web application development. Here's to pushing the boundaries, embracing innovation, and creating digital experiences that leave a lasting impression.

Happy coding!

Preface

Interactive Web Application Development Angular and Typescript covers: Introduction to Angular and Typescript.

AngularJS, not to be confused with its successor Angular (which dropped the "JS" for simplicity), is a front-end framework that's all about making your web applications more dynamic and interactive. It's like giving your static HTML a shot of adrenaline, allowing you to create single-page applications with ease.

One of the standout features is two-way data binding. Think of it as a magical connection between your application's model and view. When the model changes, so does the view, and vice versa. It's like having a real-time conversation between your data and your user interface.

Directives are another cool aspect of AngularJS. These are like little nuggets of HTML awesomeness that extend the functionality of your elements. Want to loop through an array and display each item? There's a directive for that! Need to hide or show elements dynamically? Yep, there's a directive for that too.

And let's not forget dependency injection. AngularJS makes it a breeze to manage your application's components and their dependencies, promoting modular and maintainable code.

With TypeScript, you get to declare types for your variables, functions, and more. It's like giving your code a roadmap, making it easier to understand and maintain. Plus, the autocompletion and intelligent suggestions in your code editor become your trusty sidekicks, helping you navigate your codebase with finesse.

Whether you're a seasoned developer or just starting your coding journey, TypeScript is there to bring a bit of order to the sometimes chaotic world of web development. So, are you ready to suit up and dive into the world of TypeScript?

Project Files and TypeScript Compilation:

In the world of TypeScript, you don't just write your code in a single file and hope for the best. Oh no, you organize your project into a harmonious collection of files. These files could include your TypeScript source code, configuration files, and maybe even some static assets.

At the heart of it all is the tsconfig.json file. This is your project's maestro, conducting the TypeScript orchestra. It holds the configuration for your TypeScript compilation, telling the compiler how to transform your TypeScript code into plain JavaScript. You can specify things like the target version of JavaScript, module systems, and where the compiled code should go.

Now, when it's showtime, you hit the TypeScript compiler with a command (maybe a friendly tsc in your terminal), and it springs into action, reading your tsconfig.json and orchestrating the conversion of your TypeScript code into JavaScript.

Components Templates Services Directives:

Components: The Leading Actors Components are the rockstars of your user interface. They encapsulate the logic and UI of a specific part of your application. It's like having mini superheroes, each responsible for their own little corner of the screen. Angular and other front-end frameworks love organizing things this way—it keeps the codebase clean and makes it easier to manage.

Templates: The Script Think of templates as the script for your components. They define how the component should look and behave. With HTML and special template syntax, you're crafting the scenes and dialogues for your components. It's the visual part of the show, dictating how the users experiences your application.

Services: The Support Crew Services are the behind-the-scenes MVPs. They handle the business logic, data fetching, and other heavy lifting that your components shouldn't be bothered with. Want to fetch data from a server, manage authentication, or handle a global state? Services got your back.

Directives: The Special Effects Directives add that extra flair to your components. They are like special effects in a movie, enhancing the visuals and behavior of your HTML elements. Want to show or hide an element dynamically, iterate over a list, or create reusable components?

Data Rendering and Events Handling: Data rendering is like giving life to your characters (data) on the screen. Your components, fueled by data from services, use their templates to display information dynamically. It's the difference between a static webpage and a dynamic, ever-changing user interface. Imagine updating a user profile picture or displaying a list of the latest movies—data rendering is what makes it happen.

Event handling is where you script the interactions between your users and the application. Clicking a button, submitting a form, or hovering over an image—these are the cues that trigger actions in your components.

Building Reusable Components: Break down your UI into modular components, each responsible for a specific task or feature. By passing data to components, you make them flexible and reusable across various parts of your application. Using event emitters and outputs, your components can signal changes or trigger actions in the parent components or even the entire application.

Controlling Rendering of HTML: Sometimes you want certain elements to steal the spotlight only under specific conditions. Using directives like *ngIf in Angular, you decide when a component or element takes center stage and when it gracefully bows out. List rendering allows you to iterate over arrays or lists and dynamically create elements for each item. With directives like *ngFor in Angular, you can showcase a dynamic list of items without hardcoding each one. Attribute binding lets you dynamically change an element's attributes based on your application's state. Whether it's altering the class for styling or updating the source of an image. Style and class binding allow you to dynamically apply styles and classes to your HTML elements. This is handy when you want to change the look and feel of your components based on user interactions or application state. When your application has multiple scenes and each requires a different setup, ngSwitch in Angular can be your directorial magic. It's like changing the entire set based on a condition, ensuring a smooth transition between different views or states.

Template Driven Forms: With template-driven forms, your HTML template is in control. No need for elaborate TypeScript code to manage form logic; instead, directives like ngModel and ngForm empower your template to handle form-related tasks. ngModel enables two-way data binding. When the user types in an input field, the template updates the component, and vice versa. It's a synchronization of user input and application state.

You can easily add validation checks directly in your template, creating a visually pleasing and user-friendly experience. Angular provides CSS classes like ng-valid and ng-invalid to style your forms based on their validation status.

ngForm orchestrates the entire form. It captures the form's state, validity, and submission status, allowing you to conduct operations like submitting the form or resetting it with ease.

With event binding, you can catch the form's ngSubmit event and trigger the desired action in your component.

Model Driven Forms: Unlike template-driven forms, model-driven forms put your TypeScript code at the forefront. You create a form model in your component, defining the structure and behavior of your form. The FormBuilder service in Angular assists in constructing your form model with ease. You use it to build form controls, groups, and arrays, setting the structure of your form. You define rules for your form controls, ensuring that the user input meets specific criteria.

Observables: In Angular, observables are heavily used for handling asynchronous operations. Things like HTTP requests, user interactions, and real-time updates are often represented as observables. The Angular framework itself is designed with observables in mind, making them a fundamental part of the development experience.

Communicating with Server with Spotify API:

Start by creating an Angular service that will communicating with the Spotify API. This service will encapsulate the logic for making HTTP requests and handling the API responses. Utilize Angular's HttpClient to send HTTP requests to the Spotify API. You might want to create methods in your service for different API endpoints, such as searching for tracks, artists, or albums. Spotify's API requires authentication. You'll need to obtain an access token by following Spotify's authentication process. Typically, you'd use OAuth 2.0 to get a token, and then include it in your requests. In your Angular component, inject the Spotify service and subscribe to the observable returned by your API request. Once the data arrives, you're free to design the encore! Display the track information in your component, update your UI, or take any other action based on the API response.

Building Single Page Application with Routing: Building a Single Page Application (SPA) with routing in Angular is like crafting a choose-your-own-adventure book where users navigate seamlessly through different chapters without reloading the entire story. Start by creating a new Angular project using the Angular CLI. Identify the different "pages" or views in your SPA and create a component for each. Use the Angular CLI to generate components. Set up the routing module to define the navigation paths and associate them with your components. Create a file named app-routing.module.ts. Import the RouterModule and AppRoutingModule in your main app.module.ts file. Also, include the router-outlet in your template to act as the placeholder for the components. Use the routerLink directive to navigate between pages in your navigation menu or within your components. Clicking on a link will dynamically load the associated component without a full page reload. Leverage Angular's router events to handle additional tasks when navigating, like updating the page title or executing specific actions. Inject the Router service into your component and subscribe to events. For larger SPAs, consider lazy loading to load modules only when needed. This improves initial load times by only fetching the necessary code when a specific route is accessed.

CRUDE with Firebase: CRUD (Create, Read, Update, Delete) operations with Firebase? Seamlessly interact with a real-time NoSQL database. Create a simple Angular application that performs CRUD operations using Firebase. Start by creating a Firebase project on the Firebase Console. Follow the steps to create a new project and set up Firebase in your Angular app. Install the Firebase SDK and AngularFire in your Angular project. Set up Firebase in your Angular app by adding your Firebase configuration in the environments files (environment.prod.ts and environment.ts). Generate a service that will handle your CRUD operations. Use the Firebase service in your Angular components to perform CRUD operations. Display the data in your component's template. You can use Angular directives like *ngFor to iterate through the items and show them on the page.

Users can add, retrieve, update, and delete data in real-time. Enjoy the magic of Firebase and Angular working together!

Acknowledgements

This endeavor, exploring the intricacies of interactive web application development with Angular and TypeScript, has been a collaborative effort enriched by the generosity and support of many remarkable individuals.

Heartfelt appreciation to family and friends for their unwavering support and encouragement. Your belief in our journey fueled the passion and dedication poured into this project.

A special thank you to those who dedicated their time to review and test the material. Your meticulous feedback played a pivotal role in refining the content, ensuring its clarity and practicality.

To the vibrant communities surrounding Angular and TypeScript, your collective knowledge and enthusiasm have been a constant source of inspiration. The open exchange of ideas and collaboration within these communities is truly empowering.

A sincere thank you to the readers and learners who embark on this educational journey. Your curiosity and commitment to mastering Angular and TypeScript drive the purpose of this book, and I hope it becomes a valuable resource in your learning path.

The magic of Angular and TypeScript is deeply indebted to the countless open-source contributors. Your collaborative spirit and dedication to advancing web development technologies have laid the foundation for the content explored in this book.

Prologue

In the ever-evolving landscape of web development, crafting interactive and dynamic user experiences has become both an art and a necessity. As the digital canvas expands, developers seek tools that empower them to build not just websites but living, breathing applications that engage and delight users.

Welcome to "Interactive Web Application Development Angular and TypeScript." This book is a compass for those navigating the vast realm of modern web development, providing a hands-on guide to mastering the powerful duo of Angular and TypeScript.

A Symphony of Technologies: Angular and TypeScript

Angular, a robust and feature-rich front-end framework, and TypeScript, a superset of JavaScript with static typing, combine forces to redefine how we conceive and build web applications. Together, they offer a structured and scalable approach to creating applications that go beyond static content and invite users to participate in a dynamic conversation.

What Awaits You in These Pages:

Foundations of Angular and TypeScript: We'll begin our journey by laying a solid foundation. Understanding the core concepts of Angular and TypeScript will empower you to wield these tools with confidence. From components and templates to services and directives, we'll dive deep into the building blocks that form the backbone of modern web applications.

Navigating the Single Page Application (SPA) Landscape: The concept of Single Page Applications has revolutionized user experiences. We'll explore the art of building SPAs with Angular's powerful routing system, allowing users to seamlessly navigate between different sections of your application without the need for page reloads.

The Dance of Data and Events: Dynamic applications are powered by the dance of data rendering and event handling. Discover how to elegantly bind data to your templates, respond to user interactions, and create a fluid user experience.

Building Reusable Components: Like skilled actors in a theatrical production, components play a central role in your application's performance. Learn the art of building reusable components that not only streamline development but also enhance the maintainability of your codebase.

Controlling the Rendering of HTML: Become the director of your HTML production. Explore techniques for conditionally rendering elements, iterating through lists, and dynamically updating styles and attributes based on your application's state.

Forms, Forms, Forms: Master the creation and management of both template-driven and model-driven forms. Uncover the secrets of capturing user input, validating data, and crafting forms that seamlessly integrate with your application's logic.

Observable Magic: Enter the world of observables, the rockstars of asynchronous programming in Angular. Learn how to manage and respond to asynchronous events, creating responsive and real-time applications.

Interacting with the Server: Harness the power of Firebase to perform CRUD operations seamlessly. Witness the integration of Firebase, Angular, and TypeScript in building applications that interact with a real-time NoSQL database.

As you embark on this exploration, remember that every chapter is a step towards mastering the craft of interactive web application development. Whether you're a seasoned developer seeking to enhance your skills or a newcomer eager to delve into the dynamic world of web development, this book is your guide.

CHAPTER ONE

Introduction - Angular and Typescript

Introduction to Angular and Typescript how to render the data and handle event as well as how to build reusable component, how to control the rendering of HTML we'll also try to design the template driven from also looking at model driven from then will be introducing observables then we will try to connect to the server and the build single page application SPA with routing as well as we structuring the large application will different modules and finally last looking at the last CRUD operation that is nothing but the Create Read Update Delete with Realtime firebase in Angular

So, in this first chapter looking at the introduction to angular and typescript in which we look

- What is Angular?
- The architecture of Angular Apps or Angular Application
- How to configure the machine to run Angular Application form where you will get the tools for designing application in Angular the

We will create our first Angular Application in this first chapter let first discuss that

1.1 What is Angular?

Angular is framework for building Java script heavy application, it is used to build SPA basically spa called Single Page Application by using angular you can simply design Single Page Application. In Angular, application are categories into two parts i.e., SPA (Single Page Application) and SWA (Standard Web Application)

SPA – Single Page Application

- SPA Stand for single page application.
- In SPA instead of reloading the whole page only the content which we have requested is reloaded.
- Using SPA, we can build fast and fluid experience for the user.
- Example – Email (Email load requested content and remaining content remain as it is).

SWA – Standard Web Application

- SWA stand for Standard Web Application.
- In SWA if we click on the reload then the whole page is reloaded.
- Example – Amazon shopping

Along with angular there are other frameworks which provide similar functionality but there are some advantages of angular than other and why we are using angular instead of another frameworks.

Advantages of Angular and Why we use it instead of another Framework......

- Angular is a leading framework and it is being around for a quiet few year. Angular is developed by Misko Hevery and Adam Abron's in 2009. Currently Angular is handle by google.
- Angular has huge community support and as a developer it is more demanding in job from angular, we can make our carrier in developer.

- In angular we will be using Typescript as a language.

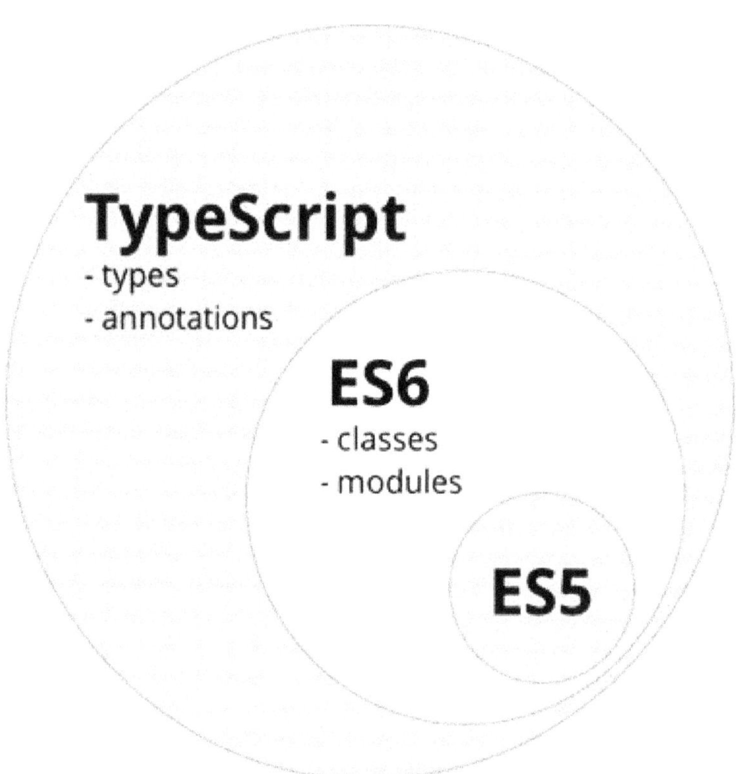

1.2 Typescript

- In the development of angular application, we are using TypeScript as a language instead of JavaScript
- A language JavaScript is supported by ES5 and ES6 with some additional features, **ES5** and **ES6** both have another subsequent version of 2016,2017, 2018,2019, 2021 and so on.
- **ES** stand for **ECMA script** which is nonprofit organization developer standard in computer hardware. It is an NGO for memory for Merly it is known as European Computer Manufacturer Association and it is an organization develop, standard in computer hardware communication and programming language it is also gives standard for JavaScript
- ES5 was introduced in year 2009 whileES6 in 2015
- ES5 support primitive data such as string, Boolean, null as well as undefined while there are some additional features in JavaScript datatypes supporting unique symbol values.
- In case of ES5 there are only one way to define variable by using VAR keyword while in ES6 there are two different new ways fir defining variables such as lit and constant using const

- ES5 has lower performance than ES6
- ES5 object manipulation is time consuming boot function and written keyword are uses to define function.
- In ES6 arrow function is a new feature by which we do not require function keyword to define function.
- ES5 provide large number of community support but currently it is also available for ES6
- ECMA has given these standards so this ES6 is major update in JavaScript language which has been released in 2015 by ECMA by providing many powerful additions to the language such as arrow function classes generator proximity and modules.
- Es6 with new version es6 2016 bring with array, prototype include ES6 2017 has a sync and evade a bit.ES6 2018 adds new capabilities to regular expression and a sync iteration or iteratorES6 2019 has object forms entries array prototype flat map ES6 2020 has dynamic input and global this even begin integer.
- Basically, typescript is not directly supported by web browsers We need to convert it into JavaScript code and that will run it into web browser.
- The typescript has modules classes Integrated access modifier like private and public we can catch many programming errors during compile time.
- These features are not supported by JavaScript so most of the angular developers prefer Typescript language for developing angular application
- Typescript is not directly use in any web browser it will have to firstly convert into a compatible js code.
- We will develop client server application and that do not require any server-side support for its execution it can be executed in any browser like Google Chrome for executing this client server angular application.

1.3 Architecture of Angular Application

There are four key layer or parts of angular application

1. Components
2. Directives
3. Routers
4. Services

Components

It is a very core of angular it encapsulates the element and template data as well as the behavior of view, it is a view component if we want to build an application like e-commerce applications like Amazon, Flipkart etc. We can active components search bar, slide bar or product.

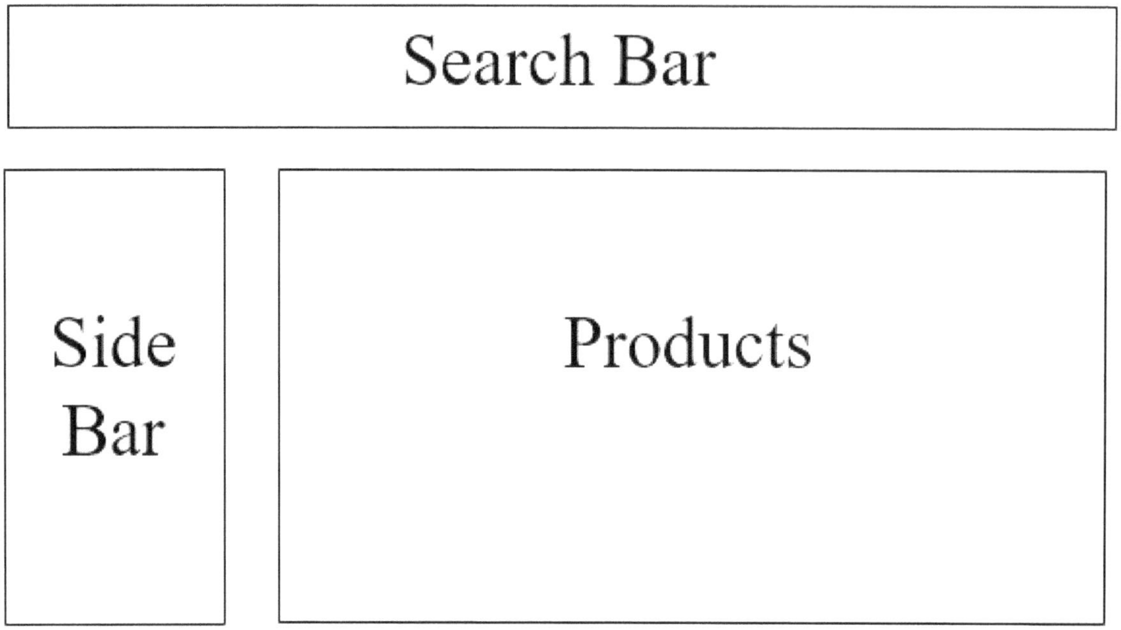

Search Bar

Side Bar

Products

Real time application can contain lots of component and each component have their own HTML marker as well as it has its own data margin, component can also contain other components. This architecture helps us to break a large application into smaller and manageable component this component is basically TypeScript class code for example we have class of product component this can be defined as

```
export class productcomponent
{
averageRating: number
setRating(value){
............................
}}
```

This is class productcomponent export here, it has various properties and method properties that are nothing but the content data and method are the function, it implements behavior of data.

Services

Service can be used to get data or to store data and save data. Component will communicate with server to get or save to store data from the server HTTP calls, logging and business rules all these services are related to user interface.

A service is typically a class with a narrow, well-defined purpose. It should do something specific and do it well.

There is nothing specifically *Angular* about services. Angular has no definition of a service. There is no service base class, and no place to register a service. Yet services are fundamental to any Angular application. Components are big consumers of services.

Router

Router is used responsible for navigation or it can establish path between all the component or pages. As well navigate one page from another it will figure out which component present to the user based on the changes in router.

Directives

Directives work with the frame that is DOM. DOM stand for Documents Objects Modules, we used directives to add behaviours for that we have HTML tag as inputs tag and adding directives as autoGrow. Input tag given by using slash (/).

```
<input type = “text” autoGrow/>
```

Angular has a bunch of directives for common type task like adding or removing DOM elements.
We can create our own custom directives.

1.4 Installation

NodeJS Installation

We need to install NodeJS, it is server-side language and we don't need it because we are not writing any server-side code. We mostly need it because of its npm or node package manager

- Visit https://nodejs.org/en/
- According to your system as window/mac/Linux download a latest or current version
- After downloading install NodeJS

Typescript Installation

We will be using typescript for our angular development

- Open command prompt in window or in Linux/Mac open terminal
- Use command

-npm install -g typescript in **Window** (*with -g we specified installation at globally. The same applies for other installations.*)
-sudo npm install -g typescript in **Linux/Mac**

Typings Installation

It is a module that allow us to bring JavaScript libraries into typescript

- Open command prompt in window or in Linux/Mac open terminal
- Use command

-npm install -g typings in **Window**
-sudo npm install -g typings in **Linux/Mac**

Angular CLI Installation

Angular CLI (Command Line Interface). It is a tool which is supported by angular which make project in simple form and it makes much easier.

- Open command prompt in window or in Linux/Mac open terminal
- Use command

-npm install -g angular-cli in **Window**
-sudo npm install -g angular-cli in **Linux/Mac**

Typescript Editor Installation

For editing code that support typescript for that we will install VScode

- Visit https://code.visualstudio.com/
- According to your system as window/mac/Linux download a latest or current version
- After downloading set-up, it

Chrome Browser

Finally, to run typescript/angular application.

After the installation and all setup firstly, we need to navigate a folder where we want save our project and after the folder selection, we will create a new angular project using following command in command prompt.

ng new Project Name .... here you can provide any name to your project in this I rename it as Angular Project (ng refer to Angular CLI or Angular Command Line Interface tool)

```
C:\Users\Lenovo\Desktop\Angular>ng new Angular_project
Node.js version v19.0.1 detected.
Odd numbered Node.js versions will not enter LTS status and should not be used
tion. For more information, please see https://nodejs.org/en/about/releases/.
? Would you like to add Angular routing? (y/N)
```

We will get the above interface in cmd after running the command **ng new** Project Name for creating our project folder the it will ask would you like to add Angular routing? simply we will go with yes. After it will ask which stylesheet format would you like to use among the four stylesheet

- CSS
- SCSS
- Sass
- Less

```
C:\Users\Lenovo\Desktop\Angular>ng new Angular_project
Node.js version v19.0.1 detected.
Odd numbered Node.js versions will not enter LTS status and should not be used
tion. For more information, please see https://nodejs.org/en/about/releases/.
? Would you like to add Angular routing? Yes
? Which stylesheet format would you like to use? (Use arrow keys)
> CSS
  SCSS   [ https://sass-lang.com/documentation/syntax#scss                ]
  Sass   [ https://sass-lang.com/documentation/syntax#the-indented-syntax ]
  Less   [ http://lesscss.org                                             ]
```

Among the four stylesheet we will go with SCSS after selecting the packages will be going to install in the selected folder

```
CREATE Angular_project/tsconfig.app.json (287 bytes)
CREATE Angular_project/tsconfig.spec.json (333 bytes)
CREATE Angular_project/.vscode/extensions.json (130 bytes)
CREATE Angular_project/.vscode/launch.json (474 bytes)
CREATE Angular_project/.vscode/tasks.json (938 bytes)
CREATE Angular_project/src/favicon.ico (948 bytes)
CREATE Angular_project/src/index.html (300 bytes)
CREATE Angular_project/src/main.ts (372 bytes)
CREATE Angular_project/src/polyfills.ts (2338 bytes)
CREATE Angular_project/src/styles.scss (80 bytes)
CREATE Angular_project/src/test.ts (749 bytes)
CREATE Angular_project/src/assets/.gitkeep (0 bytes)
CREATE Angular_project/src/environments/environment.prod.ts (51 bytes)
CREATE Angular_project/src/environments/environment.ts (658 bytes)
CREATE Angular_project/src/app/app-routing.module.ts (245 bytes)
CREATE Angular_project/src/app/app.module.ts (393 bytes)
CREATE Angular_project/src/app/app.component.html (23115 bytes)
CREATE Angular_project/src/app/app.component.spec.ts (1100 bytes)
CREATE Angular_project/src/app/app.component.ts (220 bytes)
CREATE Angular_project/src/app/app.component.scss (0 bytes)
- Installing packages (npm)...
```

After installation of all packages we will se the message as packages installed successfully as show in following image.

```
CREATE Angular_project/.vscode/launch.json (474 bytes)
CREATE Angular_project/.vscode/tasks.json (938 bytes)
CREATE Angular_project/src/favicon.ico (948 bytes)
CREATE Angular_project/src/index.html (300 bytes)
CREATE Angular_project/src/main.ts (372 bytes)
CREATE Angular_project/src/polyfills.ts (2338 bytes)
CREATE Angular_project/src/styles.scss (80 bytes)
CREATE Angular_project/src/test.ts (749 bytes)
CREATE Angular_project/src/assets/.gitkeep (0 bytes)
CREATE Angular_project/src/environments/environment.prod.ts (51 bytes)
CREATE Angular_project/src/environments/environment.ts (658 bytes)
CREATE Angular_project/src/app/app-routing.module.ts (245 bytes)
CREATE Angular_project/src/app/app.module.ts (393 bytes)
CREATE Angular_project/src/app/app.component.html (23115 bytes)
CREATE Angular_project/src/app/app.component.spec.ts (1100 bytes)
CREATE Angular_project/src/app/app.component.ts (220 bytes)
CREATE Angular_project/src/app/app.component.scss (0 bytes)
√ Packages installed successfully.
'git' is not recognized as an internal or external command,
operable program or batch file.

C:\Users\Lenovo\Desktop\Angular>
```

For running our angular application, we must open the project folder where we have created with name Angular_project by simply typing command ng serve after opening it will ask would you like to share pseudonymous usage data about this project with angular team at Google under

```
C:\>cd C:\Users\Lenovo\Desktop\Angular\Angular_project

C:\Users\Lenovo\Desktop\Angular\Angular_project>ng serve
Node.js version v19.0.1 detected.
Odd numbered Node.js versions will not enter LTS status and should not be used for produc
tion. For more information, please see https://nodejs.org/en/about/releases/.
? Would you like to share pseudonymous usage data about this project with the Angular
Team
at Google under Google's Privacy Policy at https://policies.google.com/privacy. For more
details and how to change this setting, see https://angular.io/analytics. (y/N)
```

Google's privacy policy. We simply allow that message and after that it will process our angular application and enabled some ng analytics after that our application will generate browser application bundles

```
C:\>cd C:\Users\Lenovo\Desktop\Angular\Angular_project

C:\Users\Lenovo\Desktop\Angular\Angular_project>ng serve
Node.js version v19.0.1 detected.
Odd numbered Node.js versions will not enter LTS status and should not be used for product
ion. For more information, please see https://nodejs.org/en/about/releases/.
? Would you like to share pseudonymous usage data about this project with the Angular
Team
at Google under Google's Privacy Policy at https://policies.google.com/privacy. For more
details and how to change this setting, see https://angular.io/analytics. Yes

Thank you for sharing pseudonymous usage data. Should you change your mind, the followingc
ommand will disable this feature entirely:

    ng analytics disable

Global setting: enabled
Local setting: enabled
Effective status: enabled
- Generating browser application bundles (phase: setup)...
```

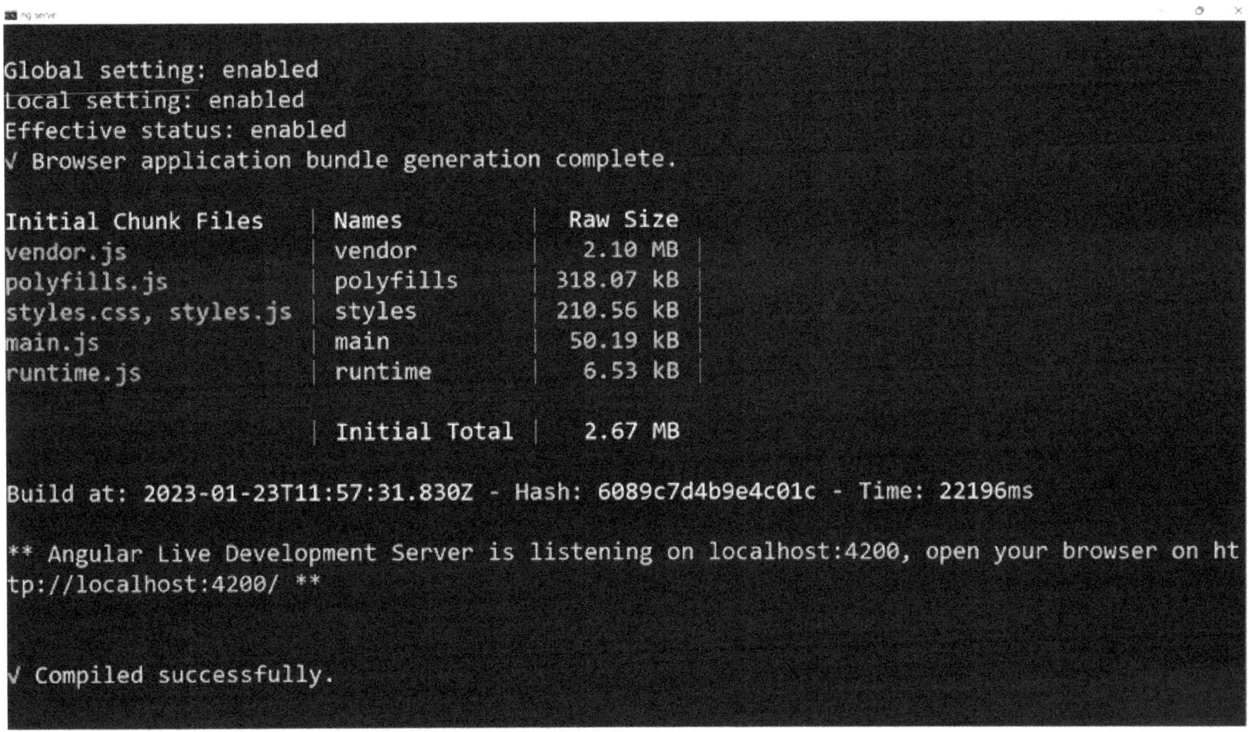

After completion, we get the above interface and our angular live development server is listening on localhost:4200. We must open this http://localhost:4200 link in chrome browser to view our project and it will look like as below and our angular application project is ready at the first stage.

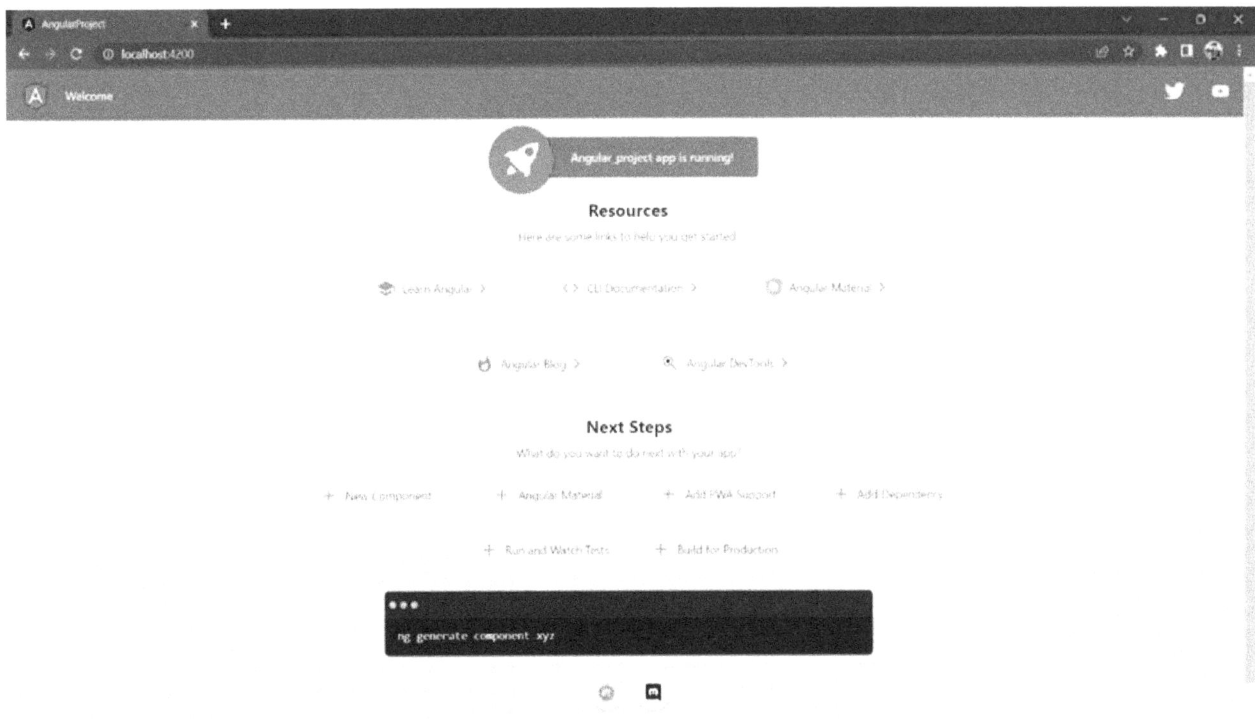

CHAPTER TWO

Project Files and TypeScript Compilation

Welcome to the Second chapter on angular and typescript. In previous Chapter we have seen what is angular, what is typescript, architecture of angular apps. We also seen the Various tools required for running your angular application which has been written in typescript. We also seen the difference between JavaScript and typescript, we discussed about **SPA** like a single page applications and **web pages** as well as we have configured our machine for running angular application so we have created our first angular project.

2.1 Overview

In this chapter we are discussing below points :-

Angular Project Files, TypeScript Compilation, Transpile, watch mode compilation, tsconfig.json, package.json, main.ts, app folder, app.module.ts, app.component.ts, app.component.html, app.component.css, app.component.scss

In this chapter will be discussing the project files that have been created when we have created our first project so in previous Chapter we have created project by executing command Ng that is nothing but the NG referred to the angular CLI that is angular command line interface in front of NG we have specified new keyword and after that I specified the name of project and when we have executed that command that is NG under our my project folder various files has been created. As shown in following screenshots:

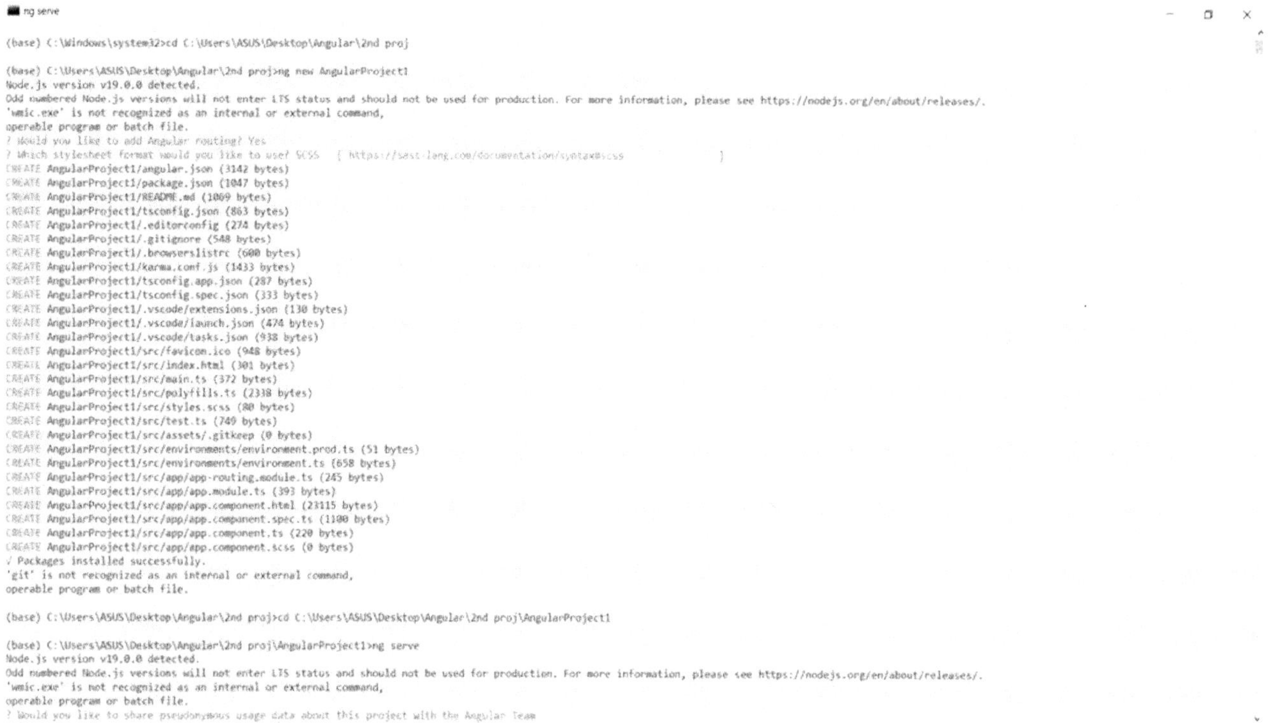

```
ng serve

(base) C:\Windows\system32>cd C:\Users\ASUS\Desktop\Angular\2nd proj

(base) C:\Users\ASUS\Desktop\Angular\2nd proj>ng new AngularProject1
Node.js version v19.0.0 detected.
Odd numbered Node.js versions will not enter LTS status and should not be used for production. For more information, please see https://nodejs.org/en/about/releases/.
'wmic.exe' is not recognized as an internal or external command,
operable program or batch file.
? Would you like to add Angular routing? Yes
? Which stylesheet format would you like to use? SCSS   [ https://sass-lang.com/documentation/syntax#scss           ]
CREATE AngularProject1/angular.json (3142 bytes)
CREATE AngularProject1/package.json (1047 bytes)
CREATE AngularProject1/README.md (1069 bytes)
CREATE AngularProject1/tsconfig.json (863 bytes)
CREATE AngularProject1/.editorconfig (274 bytes)
CREATE AngularProject1/.gitignore (548 bytes)
CREATE AngularProject1/.browserslistrc (600 bytes)
CREATE AngularProject1/karma.conf.js (1433 bytes)
CREATE AngularProject1/tsconfig.app.json (287 bytes)
CREATE AngularProject1/tsconfig.spec.json (333 bytes)
CREATE AngularProject1/.vscode/extensions.json (130 bytes)
CREATE AngularProject1/.vscode/launch.json (474 bytes)
CREATE AngularProject1/.vscode/tasks.json (938 bytes)
CREATE AngularProject1/src/favicon.ico (948 bytes)
CREATE AngularProject1/src/index.html (301 bytes)
CREATE AngularProject1/src/main.ts (372 bytes)
CREATE AngularProject1/src/polyfills.ts (2338 bytes)
CREATE AngularProject1/src/styles.scss (80 bytes)
CREATE AngularProject1/src/test.ts (749 bytes)
CREATE AngularProject1/src/assets/.gitkeep (0 bytes)
CREATE AngularProject1/src/environments/environment.prod.ts (51 bytes)
CREATE AngularProject1/src/environments/environment.ts (658 bytes)
CREATE AngularProject1/src/app/app-routing.module.ts (245 bytes)
CREATE AngularProject1/src/app/app.module.ts (393 bytes)
CREATE AngularProject1/src/app/app.component.html (23115 bytes)
CREATE AngularProject1/src/app/app.component.spec.ts (1100 bytes)
CREATE AngularProject1/src/app/app.component.ts (220 bytes)
CREATE AngularProject1/src/app/app.component.scss (0 bytes)
√ Packages installed successfully.
'git' is not recognized as an internal or external command,
operable program or batch file.

(base) C:\Users\ASUS\Desktop\Angular\2nd proj>cd C:\Users\ASUS\Desktop\Angular\2nd proj\AngularProject1

(base) C:\Users\ASUS\Desktop\Angular\2nd proj\AngularProject1>ng serve
Node.js version v19.0.0 detected.
Odd numbered Node.js versions will not enter LTS status and should not be used for production. For more information, please see https://nodejs.org/en/about/releases/.
'wmic.exe' is not recognized as an internal or external command,
operable program or batch file.
? Would you like to share pseudonymous usage data about this project with the Angular Team
```

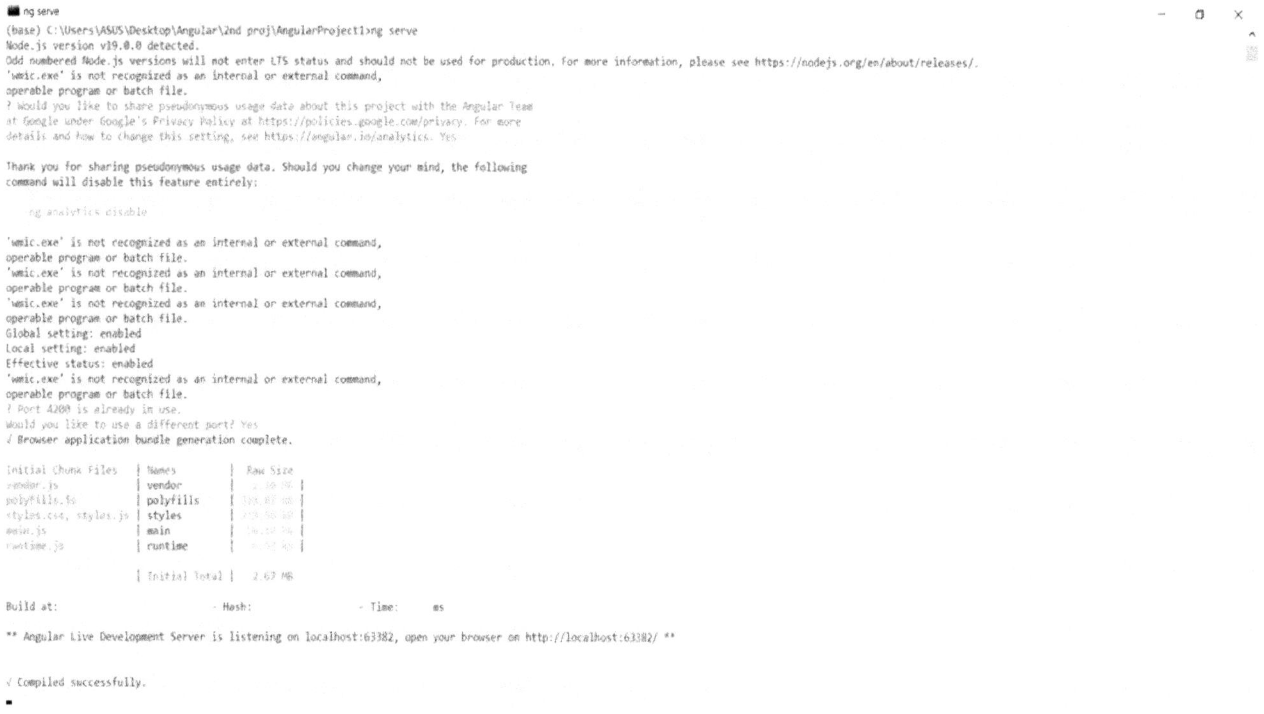

```
ng serve
(base) C:\Users\ASUS\Desktop\Angular\2nd proj\AngularProject1>ng serve
Node.js version v19.0.0 detected.
Odd numbered Node.js versions will not enter LTS status and should not be used for production. For more information, please see https://nodejs.org/en/about/releases/.
'wmic.exe' is not recognized as an internal or external command,
operable program or batch file.
? Would you like to share pseudonymous usage data about this project with the Angular Team
at Google under Google's Privacy Policy at https://policies.google.com/privacy. For more
details and how to change this setting, see https://angular.io/analytics. Yes

Thank you for sharing pseudonymous usage data. Should you change your mind, the following
command will disable this feature entirely:

    ng analytics disable

'wmic.exe' is not recognized as an internal or external command,
operable program or batch file.
'wmic.exe' is not recognized as an internal or external command,
operable program or batch file.
'wmic.exe' is not recognized as an internal or external command,
operable program or batch file.
Global setting: enabled
Local setting: enabled
Effective status: enabled
'wmic.exe' is not recognized as an internal or external command,
operable program or batch file.
? Port 4200 is already in use.
Would you like to use a different port? Yes
√ Browser application bundle generation complete.

Initial Chunk Files      | Names         |  Raw Size
vendor.js                | vendor        | [illegible] |
polyfills.js             | polyfills     | [illegible] |
styles.css, styles.js    | styles        | [illegible] |
main.js                  | main          | [illegible] |
runtime.js               | runtime       | [illegible] |

                         | Initial Total |   2.67 MB

Build at:                        - Hash:                    - Time:      ms

** Angular Live Development Server is listening on localhost:63382, open your browser on http://localhost:63382/ **


√ Compiled successfully.
```

2.2 Angular Project Files

So we'll be discussing some of the main files that will be using throughout creation of various project . In this project there are various configuration files which has been created. So initially we will open this project folder in visual Studio code (VS Code). So first time we are running this Visual Studio code so you can select and you can open your project folder that is the path of the project .so now this my first project folder has been opened and you can view all the files that has been created.

All ready created a **Source folder**. So inside source folder you have **app folder** most of the times that is 99% of the time will be editing code files inside the app folder so in the source folder we have this **main.ts** file.

2.3 TypeScript Compilation

The TypeScript compiler compiles these files and outputs the JavaScript with . js extension by keeping the same file name as the individual input file so **.ts** indicates the typescript so this main.ts is nothing but the starting model for our angular application. So basically you can see just like in Java programming language you have main function in a C programming language you have main function right in similar manner this main.ts is a starting model for your angular application. So in this project folder you can find this tsconfig.json file. this is the configuration file for the typescript compiler.

We are using times typescript language here instead of JavaScript but as discussed in previous chapter your browser cannot directly execute typescript. So it should be converted into JavaScript so this process is called as **transpile.**

Basically the typescript compiler convert your typescript file into the targeted JavaScript as you can see here as in previous chapter. We have drawn one diagram where we have shown es5 and es6 & discussing all details of the **ecma.**

Ecma script has been introduced by the ecma organization so here our typescript is getting converted into JavaScript targeted JavaScript so it will be converted into es 2020 JavaScript. So the JavaScript version that will be used by the compiler the transpiles your typescript into es 2020 which is the current version of JavaScript because we have installed the latest version of node as well as typescript and to know more about this **ts** config file.

2.4 Workspace configuration files

All projects within a workspace share a CLI configuration context. The top level of the workspace contains workspace-wide configuration files, configuration files for the root-level application, and subfolders for the root-level application source and test files. The workspace configuration files and their purpose is specified below:

.editorconfig: Configuration for code editors. See EditorConfig.

.gitignore: Specifies intentionally untracked files that Git should ignore.

README.md: Introductory documentation for the root application

angular.json: CLI configuration defaults for all projects in the workspace, including configuration options for build, serve, and test tools that the CLI uses, such as Karma, and Protractor. For details, see Angular Workspace Configuration.

package.json: Configures npm package dependencies that are available to all projects in the workspace. See npm documentation for the specific format and contents of this file.

package-lock.json: Provides version information for all packages installed into node_modules by the npm client. See npm documentation for details. If you use the yarn client, this file will be yarn.lock instead.

src/: Source files for the root-level application project.

node_modules/: Provides npm packages to the entire workspace. Workspace-wide node_modules dependencies are visible to all projects.

tsconfig.json: The base TypeScript configuration for projects in the workspace. All other configuration files inherit from this base file. For more information, see the Configuration inheritance with extends section of the TypeScript documentation.

2.5 Application project files

By default, the CLI command ng new my-app creates a workspace folder named "my-app" and generates a new application skeleton in a src/ folder at the top level of the workspace. A newly generated application contains source files for a root module, with a root component and template.

2.6 Application source files

Files at the top level of src/ support testing and running your application. Subfolders contain the application source and application-specific configuration. The application source files and their purpose is specified below:

app/: Contains the component files in which your application logic and data are defined. See details below.

assets/: Contains image and other asset files to be copied as-is when you build your application.

favicon.ico: An icon to use for this application in the bookmark bar.

index.html: The main HTML page that is served when someone visits your site. The CLI automatically adds all JavaScript and CSS files when building your app, so you typically don't need to add any <script> or <link> tags here manually.

main.ts: The main entry point for your application. Compiles the application with the JIT compiler and bootstraps the application's root module (AppModule) to run in the browser. You can also use the AOT compiler without changing any code by appending the --aot flag to the CLI build and serve commands.

styles.sass: Lists CSS files that supply styles for a project. The extension reflects the style preprocessor you have configured for the project.

Inside the src folder, the app folder contains your project's logic and data. Angular components, templates, and styles go here.

app/app.component.ts: Defines the logic for the application's root component, named AppComponent. The view associated with this root component becomes the root of the view hierarchy as you add components and services to your application

app/app.component.html: Defines the HTML template associated with the root AppComponent.

app/app.component.css: Defines the base CSS stylesheet for the root AppComponent.

app/app.component.spec.ts: Defines a unit test for the root AppComponent

app/app.module.ts: Defines the root module, named AppModule, that tells Angular how to assemble the application. Initially declares only the AppComponent. As you add more components to the app, they must be declared here.

2.7 Application configuration files

The application-specific configuration files for the root application reside at the workspace root level. For a multi-project workspace, project-specific configuration files are in the project root, under projects/project-name/. Project-specific TypeScript configuration files inherit from the workspace-wide tsconfig.json. The application configuration files and their purpose is specified below:

tsconfig.app.json: Application-specific TypeScript configuration, including TypeScript and Angular template compiler options. See TypeScript Configuration and Angular Compiler Options

tsconfig.spec.json: TypeScript configuration for the application tests. See TypeScript Configuration

CHAPTER THREE

Components, Templates, Services, and Directives

In this chapter we will be discussing about creating components, using components- templates, services, and dependency injection. So, in previous chapter core building blocks of angular application which comprises or architecture of angular applications comprises components directives services and routers. In this we will implement a component rate as well as services from those four key building blocks of any angular application.

3.1 Creating Components

For creating component firstly, we will open our application in VS code editor. Now we will create the component as name product component so in VS code we have initially open the project folder which we have created. In previous chapter as we seen here all the files has been automatically created when we have created the new project with name as **Angular_Project**. In this folder we first add a new file in the app folder so our folder is located inside the src folder, in app folder we add new file name as products.component.ts, (ts indicate the typescript).

products.component.ts:

```
import {Component} from '@angular/core'
@Component ({
selector: 'products',
template: '<h2>Products</h2>'
})
export class productscomponent {
}
```

Code Explanation:

In this product.component.ts we will write code firstly import component from angular core then we including net component so we will be adding selector as products and template as using heading tag. Therefore, the decorator component is added here then we must export a class as productscomponent.

So, this ***import {component} from '@angular/core'*** import component decorator which has been imported from the core angular module, there are multiple modules in these cores angular and these are predefined module the class we are defining here is a component class. The component decorator is added whenever we are using decorator it can be used in front of the component or modules so those will be acting as functions so it can be taken object within the curly brackets, we are specifying an object with two attributes, as selector and template so these attributes are defined in this component decorator and if we observe these both having type string because we have defined both in single quotes.

This selector specifies CSS selector for a host HTML element. When angular sees an element so that this element matches the CSS selector, it will create an instance of our component in the host element. Here, our host element is an element with this tag products *<h2>Products</h2>*. Template specifies the HTML that will be inserted into the DOM when the component's view is rendered. We can either write the HTML here inline, or reference to it in a separate HTML file with the attribute templateUrl which we see in app.component.ts. Our current HTML markup is

<h2>Products</h2>.

And lastly, we have an export keyword which makes this class available for other files in our angular application so that we can import the class with product component so now we can say this is a user defined class with these simply we have created our first component. For using products.component.ts we should go inside the app.component.ts because our application will be using these products.component.ts now, we will go inside app.component.ts inside this

```
app.component.ts
import { Component } from '@angular/core';
@Component({
selector: 'app-root',
templateUrl: './app.component.html',
styleUrls: ['./app.component.scss']
})
export class AppComponent {
title = ' Angular_project ';
}
```

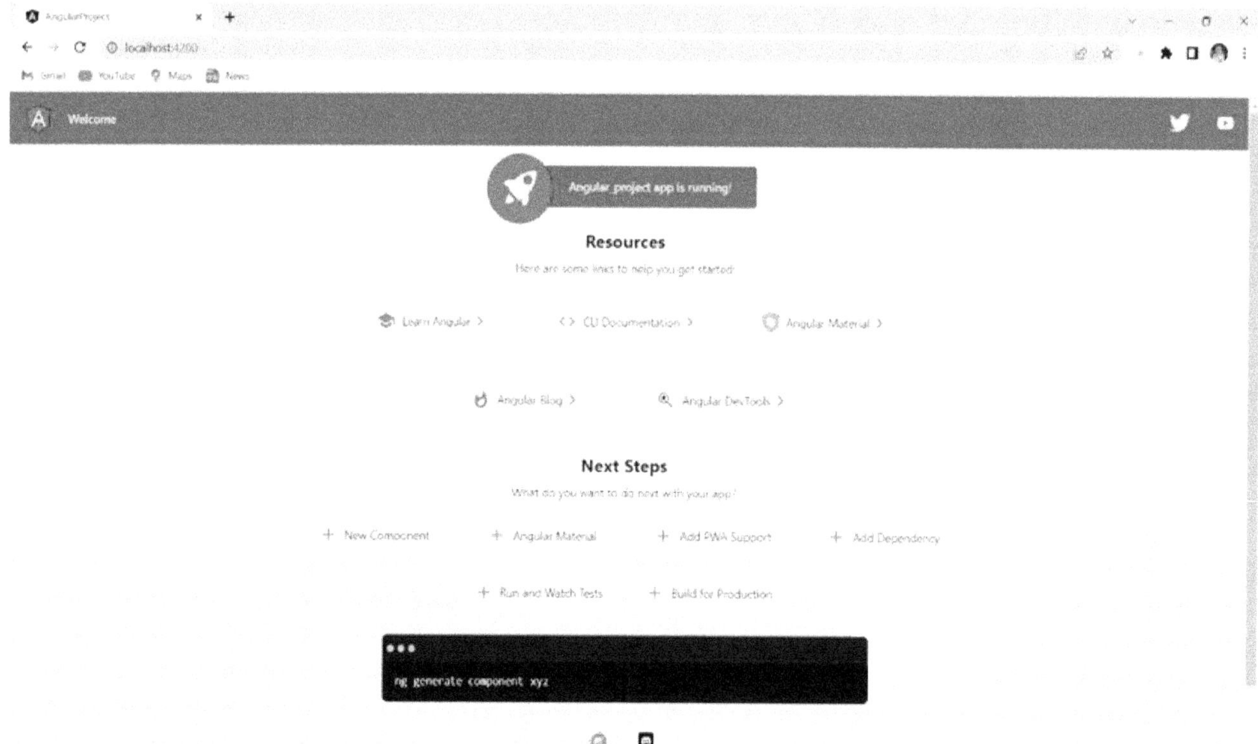

Code Explanation:

Component we can notice that app.component.ts is like products.component.ts because app.component.ts also has component which we have inserted in both component ***import {Component} from '@angular/core'*** *as* well as each component has component decorator as ***@Component***.Every Angular application has at least one component: the root component,named AppComponent in app.component.ts . Components are the basic building blocksof Angular applications. This class is decorated with the Component decorator @Component. Like the module decorator, the component decorator adds metadata above this class. Because decorators are functions, we need to use the prefix @ sign to call the @Component function with its brackets @Component(...). All components in Angular are essentially decorated TypeScript classes.

In the ***app.component.ts*** import {Component} from **'@angular/core'***as* well as each component has component decorator as ***@Component***. We also have other argument selector, templateUrl and then styleUrls. The field templateUrl we refer to our HTML markup in the separate file basically app.component.html but it is better to put it separately file using templateUrl however if html markup is not too big and it is easier to have the component.ts file as we can view all at single glance.

for example, so by changing the templateUrl to template and inserting our HTML markup in app.component.ts so instead of specifying templateUrl we can simply specify it as template and directly insert template here like <h1> tag and add ((title)) then and we will close the <h1> tag. We have directly added the markup here so, same is applied to our styleUrls but as you can see that this styleUrls referred to **app.component.scss** and it does not contain anything right we can simply remove this **app.component.scss** and remove the styleUrls. After that we delete the **app.component.html** and **app.component.scss file** because we are notusing any templateUrl or styleUrls currentlyto make our code clean and we are editing the files which we had already created in our project. Inside the **app.component.ts** we can simply modify the title of our application whatever we need and then we can observer a title which we had change it will update instantly without refreshing the page. So, after editing the title of our application code, and output look like

```
app.component.ts
import { Component } from '@angular/core';
@Component({
selector: 'app-root',
template: '<h1>{{title}}</h1>'
})
export class AppComponent {
title = 'Chapter Number 3';
}
```

Chapter Number 3

In the above image chapter Number 3 is showing as a heading that is we had earlier specified the title in the above code.

So now we'll export the ***app.component.ts*** in export class app component we remembered that ***app component*** is the root of our application and it is the view component that controls our entire app. For product component we are using selector as products so that can be used as tag and the template for tag will be inside the heading with production. So, in our app component as we are specifying the template on multiple line initially the templateUrl referring to HTML file **app.component.html**. Whatever markup was there that was displayed in the browser as the app output but currently we have deleted it and templateUrl we have removed from ***app.component.ts***. So, we are inserting the products in ***app.component.ts file*** now we are writing the HTML markup on multiple lines, so we can use the slashes used in the template attribute and also we can have backtick here. Backtick is not single code, it is a character and it is located in the top left of the keyboard, just before the number 1 (`).So, that's how we are now using products after saving it if we observe in code, that products have not been used. So, it is showing some problem in our code, for solving the problem we will edit our **app.module.ts** file. So, initially what we had done we had created the product component. Right now, this product component we want to use in our application.

3.2 Using Components

So, we have created productscomponent ***products.component.ts*** and we are using these this product components. So, for that purpose we have initially created our ***app.component.ts*** file and we are using ***products.component.ts*** inside our application but you should also specify it inside the module file so, now will be making changes in **app.module.ts.** So that will be our next step to edit **app.module.ts.** Inside the **app** folder we find the **app.module.ts** and app component it is basically using app component which has been defined in ***app.component.ts.*** So similarly, it should also use the product component. So, for that purpose now product component is different paths, so we will add product component in **app.module.ts**. So basically, for using product component user different product component will use import then we name that class as productscomponent, correct?

```
app.module.ts
import { NgModule } from '@angular/core';
import { BrowserModule } from '@angular/platform-browser';
import { AppRoutingModule } from './app-routing.module';
import { AppComponent } from './app.component';
@NgModule({
declarations: [
AppComponent
],
imports: [
BrowserModule,
AppRoutingModule
],
providers: [],
bootstrap: [AppComponent]
})
export class AppModule { }
```

Code Explanation:

So, we will be using Products component in **app.module.ts** which is user defined and it has been used from ***products.component.ts*** in the root directory of application we have ***products.component.ts*** these is how we will be using it and inside the module decorator of **app.module.ts** we have declaration for app component similarly, now we will be having declaration for Productscomponent. Now in **app.module.ts** we have two declaration that is AppComponent as well as productscomponent and we will save this. In module we have inserted and if we again observe the output now, we can see that problem which we are facing that is solved and our product component has been inserted.

Alright Back to our code if you want explanation of it so, for custom component we have defined inside ***products.component.ts.*** So, we need to specify their path in the file system. Since app component in **app.module.ts** we can see app component defined inside ***app.component.ts.*** We also have product component so both app component and product components are inside the same folder that is **app.module.ts** app and in for that purpose we used here dot slash authorize dot slash (./) so we used dot slash which means that start searching from the current folder followed by the name of the component. So, after editing ***app.module.ts*** file our code and output look like as follow

```
app.module.ts
import { NgModule } from '@angular/core';
import { FormsModule } from '@angular/forms';
import { AppComponent } from './app.component';
```

```
import { AppRoutingModule } from './app-routing.module';
import { productscomponent } from './products.component';
import { BrowserModule } from '@angular/platform-browser';
@NgModule({
declarations: [AppComponent, productscomponent],
imports: [BrowserModule, FormsModule, AppRoutingModule],
providers: [],
bootstrap: [AppComponent],
})
export class AppModule {}
```

Chapter Number 3

Products

So, in ***app.module.ts*** name of the component is the products basically. We have product component which has been specified without ***.ts*** extension. So, when we add product components in the declaration. So, basically declarations in ***app.module.ts*** is an array which is array comprising two element first one is AppComponent and second one is the productscomponent and we can say that it is a part of module. The productscomponent is the part of the current module. So, when Angular see the product tag. So, we have added that product tag ***<products></products>*** in ***app.component.ts***. See in the output initially title is there and then product tag is there, so when our angular sees the product tag Angular will load the product component for the tag which is responsible for this product because we have specified inside the module the **productscomponent.** Whenever product tag will appear there so, we can also see that the product tag is simply directive. Product derives as custom directive so, we are also looking at not only the 2 building blocks of the angular application architecture, that is component and services. We have seen templates also we have edited template; we have gone through component but now we are also looking at directives.

3.3 Directives

Directives is the third building block of the angular application architecture. So, the product tag we can simply look at ***<products></products>*** this product tag is a custom direct. In angular directive is a class that allows us to extend or control our document object model as we discussed in the previous session, we can design custom element that are not part of standard HTML. We will use the product component for that purpose we define our new element inside the product component we have defined the new element products. Every component is technically a direct right whenever you are adding any component so that can be construed as direct. So, different is that the component has template and having template but directive doesn't have any template. We will have directive in ***app.component.ts*** , but it does not have any complete. If we observe the HTML element as root element in app root, so in <approot>we have HTML element in which we have h1 element as well as product element and in h1 element we have title and product has been configured as per the our productscomponent. So, for observing these elements if we go on browser with output and inspect HTML, we can see the <approot>. If we inspect the HTML element for the code output so we can see that <approot>is present there as shown in image.

Which has been specified inside the code that is <approot>and inside <approot>we can observe that h1 tag is there. So, in inspect the HTML file there we can see that the root element is the <approot>having two child element First one is h1 that is Chapter Number 3 and second child element is the products, so products has entered the another child element as products. So, this is because our root element template has been defined as h1 and products as two child elements. This has been rendering the application component basically. So, whatever application components are there that is under app component, all those are rendered.

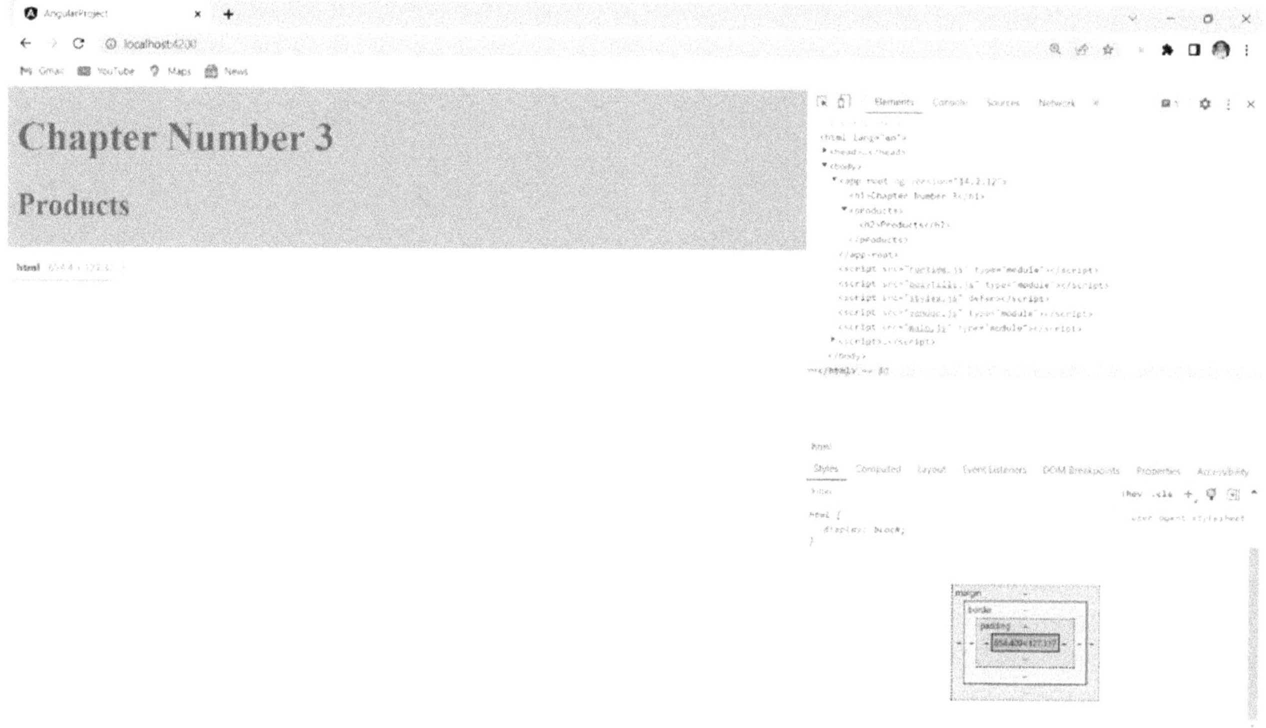

Now let us try to display a list inside this product right below this product. So, in our code that is ***products.component.ts*** we will declare one array and name that array as products and inside that product array we will be having four elements for example

- Mobile
- Smartwatch
- Laptop
- Computer

So, we can take any strings in ***products.component.ts*** inside the products array. Now we'll be changing our template so to specify a template on multiple line we have this backtick (`) character we will be displaying unorder list here, so we will be using ul tag (<ul>) and inside the ul tag we will be having list using li or <li> tag.

Now we want to iterate through this product array and no need to write down four list tag here separately. So, for that we'll be using ngFor which is basically act as for loop and in front of it I can specify product of our array name is products. So, for every element product from products array. So, from products array it will take one by one element and inside that list we will display the product.

So, product will get one by one display like first mobile will get displayed list in order list and after completing coding our code and output look like as follow

products.component.ts

```
import { Component } from '@angular/core';
@Component({
selector: 'products',
template: `
<h2>Products</h2>
<ul>
<li *ngFor="let product of products">
{{ product }}
</li>
</ul>
`,
})
export class ProductsComponent {
products = ['Mobile', 'Smartwatch', 'laptop', 'Computer'];
}
```

localhost:4200

Chapter Number 3

Products

- Mobile
- Smartwatch
- laptop
- Computer

Code Explanation:

<li *ngFor="let product of products"> allows us to repeat <li></li> for each product.

The *ngFor keyword acts like a for-loop, where we let product be the temporary local variable representing each element in the array products for each product, we use interpolation {{product}} to display the product.

Templates in Angular looks like html most of the time. Sometimes, we use special attributes like *ngFor which is an example of a directive provided by Angular. This directive extends the html and adds extra behaviour, in this case, repeating the <li> element based on the expression assigned to it.

3.4 Services and Dependency Injection

Currently, our component is rendering a hardcoded list of products. In a real-world application however, we would get the data from a server. Components should only contain logic related to the view. Logic to get data from a server should not be in a component but instead be encapsulated in a separate class called a service. We will now create a service that will get data from a server. In the app folder, create a new file called **product.service.ts**

```
product.service.ts
export class ProductService {
getProducts(): string[] {
return ['Mobile', 'Smartwatch', 'laptop', 'Computer'];
}
}
```

Code Explanation:

If you notice, a service (like a component) is just a plain class. It contains a method getProducts() of return type string array as represented by getProducts() :string[] . For now, we illustrate by returning the same hard-coded array as before so as not to get distracted by how to call a RESTful api in our service (we will discuss later in further chapter).

Dependency Injection

In **products.component.ts** , we will add the below code because we are using hard-coded array

```
export class ProductsComponent{
products;
constructor(productService: ProductService){
this.products = productService.getProducts();
}
}
```

Changing ***products.component.ts*** file code for the dependency at it look like below

products.component.ts

```
import { Component } from '@angular/core';
import { ProductService } from './product.service';
@Component({
selector: 'products',
template: `
<h2>Products</h2>
<ul>
<li *ngFor="let product of products">
{{ product }}
</li>
</ul>
`,
})
export class ProductsComponent {
//products = ['Mobile', 'Smartwatch', 'laptop', 'Computer'];
products;
constructor(productService: ProductService) {
this.products = productService.getProducts();
}
}
```

Code Explanation:

Our string array products is populated by the constructor. The constructor takes in a ProductService object. We call the getProducts() method of the ProductService object and assign the results to our products array. You might ask, how do we create the Product service and pass it into the constructor? That is when Dependency Injection which is built into Angular comes into the picture. Dependency injection injects dependencies of your classes when creating them. So when creating a ProductsComponent , it looks at the constructor and see that we need a ProductService , it will create an instance of ProductService and then inject it into the constructor of the ProductsComponent class.

At last, in **app.component.ts** , add the lines which is in underline.

```
import { Component } from '@angular/core';
import { ProductService } from './product.service';
@Component({
selector: 'app-root',
```

```
template: ` <h1>{{ title }}</h1>
<products></products>`,
providers: [ProductService],
})
export class AppComponent {
title: string = 'Chapter Number 3';
}
```

The providers array contains the dependencies of the ProductsComponent . So here, we say that ProductService is a dependency of ProductsComponent . If you run the application now, you should see the same list of products as before. Only now that we have encapsulated the data retrieval logic to ProductService and ensure that ProductsComponent contains only user-interface related logic

I am putting the following task so that you can do at your own and you can extend this application to create the component as we have created the product component you can create placements component.

CHAPTER FOUR

Data Rendering and Events Handling

In these chapter we will see about data rendering and handling events. In these we will explore different kinds of bindings in angular applications such as binding various properties of DOM elements to component properties as well as we will see how to apply CSS classes on styles dynamically and then we will see how to handle events raised from DOM elements so first we'll discuss here the property binding.

4.1 Property Binding

We have already learned about interpolation where we have display properties of component also as we have done interpolation for title so initially open our project. As In app.component.ts we have interpolated the title basically it is getting replaced with the title string that have assigned to it. Now, we will again run project. Now, we will again run this project on command prompt using ng serve now our URL is open in the browser. Now we change our title name as Data Rendering and Events Handling. Now our application is available on URL and copy paste in browser as our title for these fourth session will be change after saving the file and it will update. The interpolation can be applied to other elements like just for example. If we are using image here in template under app root you can have image tag in that parameter as src source we are specifying src in that image URL.

In interpolation basically we display the properties of component in the view, we use in these as image. For image element we can also have these to get display but before including it we will save it and changes see in the browser. We can use any imageUrl so this imageUrl can be replaced with any placeholder images just for example picsum.photos or also have lorem pixel where we have placeholder images in front of it, we have to simply specify the size of image to get display there. We can take image from our local system also. Now any random image gets displayed according to the given resolution.

We have learnt about interpolation where we display properties of a component in the view for example, <h1>{{title}}</h1>. Interpolation can also be applied to other elements like <img> to display an image in the view as shown below.

app.component.ts

```
import { Component } from '@angular/core';
@Component ({
selector: 'app-root',
template: `
<h1>{{title}}</h1>
<img src = "{{imageUrl}}"/>
`

})
export class AppComponent {
title = 'Angular_project';
imageUrl = " https://picsum.photos/seed/picsum/200/300 ";
}
```

In the code above, using interpolation, we bind the src property of our DOM element to the imageUrl property in component. When there are changes in the imageUrl property of the component, it will be reflected in the DOM. Any changes in the DOM however are not reflected in the component. This is one way binding.

There are also alternative syntaxes for binding the properties.

```
<img src="{{imageUrl}}"/>
<img [src]= "imageUrl"/>
<img bind-src="imageUrl"/>
```

For the first alternative, we put the DOM property in that DOM object model is image here and it's property is src we have put that src without brackets. In the second alternative we put DOM property in square brackets [] i.e src. For the third alternative, we prefix it with bind- . Although all three syntaxes are identical, preferably we'll using these type of syntax as

<img src="{{imageUrl}}"/> as it is one of the cleaner syntax.

4.2 CSS Class Binding

In these we show a button in our view using two bootstrap CSS classes so we will use btn and btn-primary class to make our button look more professional we'll be using this bootstrap classes. If you are not familiar with bootstrap, it is an HTML, CSS, javascript framework to help build user interface components for websites or web applications. It contains HTML and CSS based design templates for example typography, forms, buttons, navigation and other interface components, as well as optional JavaScript extensions. For now, we are interested in its templates for buttons so that it should look more professional.

So we will add one more DOM element in app.component.ts as button and here we are using class for that button we using two classes as btn and btn-primary then close it and give label for example here we using submit button so for separate closing tag is used here. All the templates or HTML source can specify here using backtick. Now save the code and check the output as submit button is displayed or not. As our code run and here is submit button which is simply displayed here there will be no action perform on it.

```
@Component({
selector: 'app-root',
template: `
<button class="btn btn-primary">Submit</button>
`
```

})

Now, we need to reference bootstrap in our index.html. So how that bootstrap can be linked so we go to the URL that is getbootstrap.com.

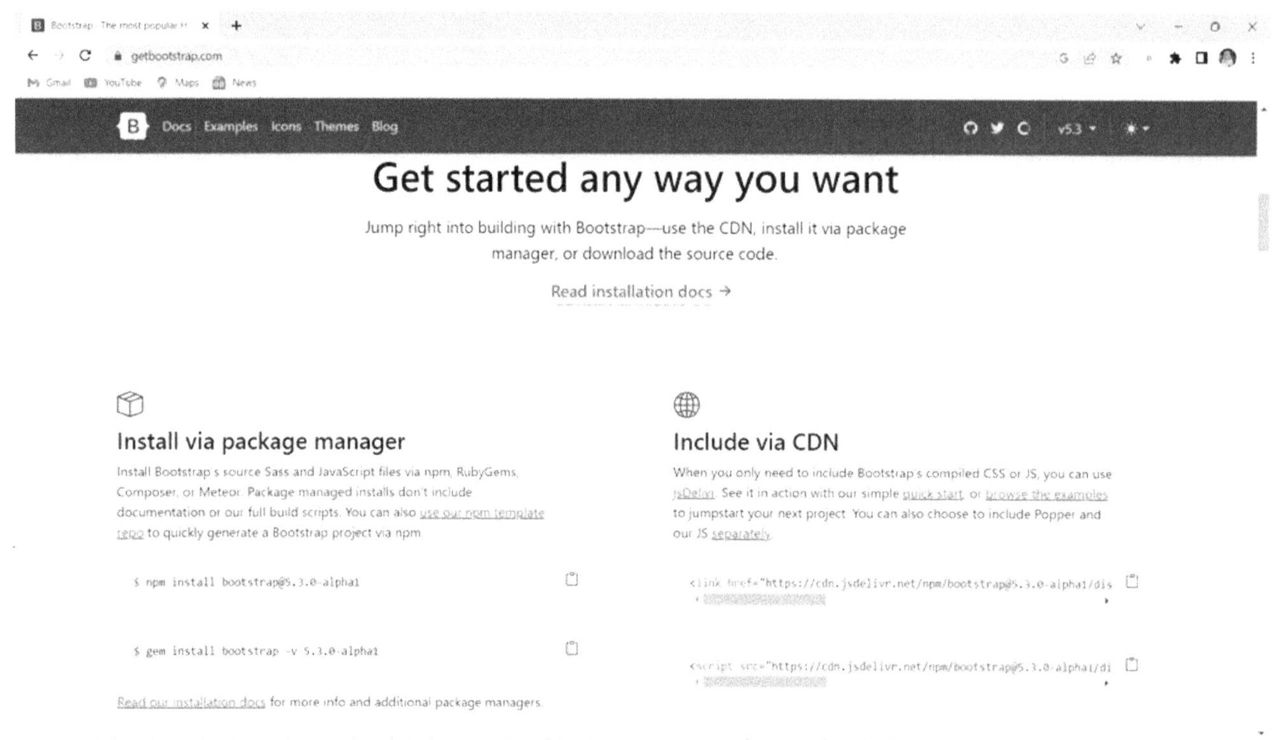

Here we will get more information on bootstrap as well as we can get the commands for installing it through node package manager(npm) we can install bootstrap with certain version at 5.2.2 and basically on bootstrap we get documentation on it. So bootstrap is a powerful extensible and feature pack front-end toolkit we can build and customize it with SAS, utilize pre-built system and components and bring projects to life with powerful javascript plugins. We can design fast responsive site with bootstrap. We must change the look of our button so for these we can copy the stylesheet link given in the include via CDN and paste it in our index.html as shown in **bold**.

index.html

<html>
<head>
<meta charset="utf-8">
<title>Chapter Number 4 </title>
<base href="/">
<meta name=" viewport" content="width=device-width, initial-scale=1">
<link rel="icon type=image/x-icon" href="favicon.ico">
<link href="https://cdn.jsdelivr.net/npm/bootstrap@5.3.0- alpha1/dist/css/bootstrap.min.css" rel="stylesheet" integrity="sha384-GLhlTQ8iRABdZLl6O3oVMWSktQOp6b7In1Zl3/Jr59b6EGGoI1aFkw7cmDA6j6gD" crossorigin="anonymous">
</head>
<body>
<app-root>Loading....</app-root>
</body>
</html>

If our code is getting successfully linked with our bootstrap then the look of our button will get changed.

There are times when we want to use different CSS classes on an element based on different conditions. For example, instead of directly using the button class as btn-primary so we also have [class.active] and if it isActive the you can have submit button here. In our app component we can specify it with semicolon this property is isActive is equals to true if frame isActive is true then it will get normally displayed.

```
@Component({
selector: 'app-root',
template: `
</button>
<button
class="btn btn-primary"
[style.backgroundColor]="isActive ? 'bule' : 'grey'"
CSSBindingSubmit
</button>
`

})
export class AppComponent {
isActive = true;
}
```

That is, when it isActive is true the CSS cloud will be applied to the button making it slightly darker and when it is false then CSS class will not be applied to the button making it lighter.

4.3 Style Binding

Style binding is a variation of property binding, similar to CSS class binding. Style binding applies inline styles to our button for example:

```
@Component({
selector: 'app-root',
template: `
<button
Class="btn btn-primary"
```

```
[style.backgroundColor]="isActive ? 'blue':'gray'">StyleBindingSubmit</button>
`

})
export class AppComponent {
isActive = true;
}
```

In app.component.ts in our component we have btn btn-primary in front of it we specified this class.active so instead of it we will change the background. If isActive is true then it will be having a blue background and if it is not active i.e isActive is false then it will display gray background.

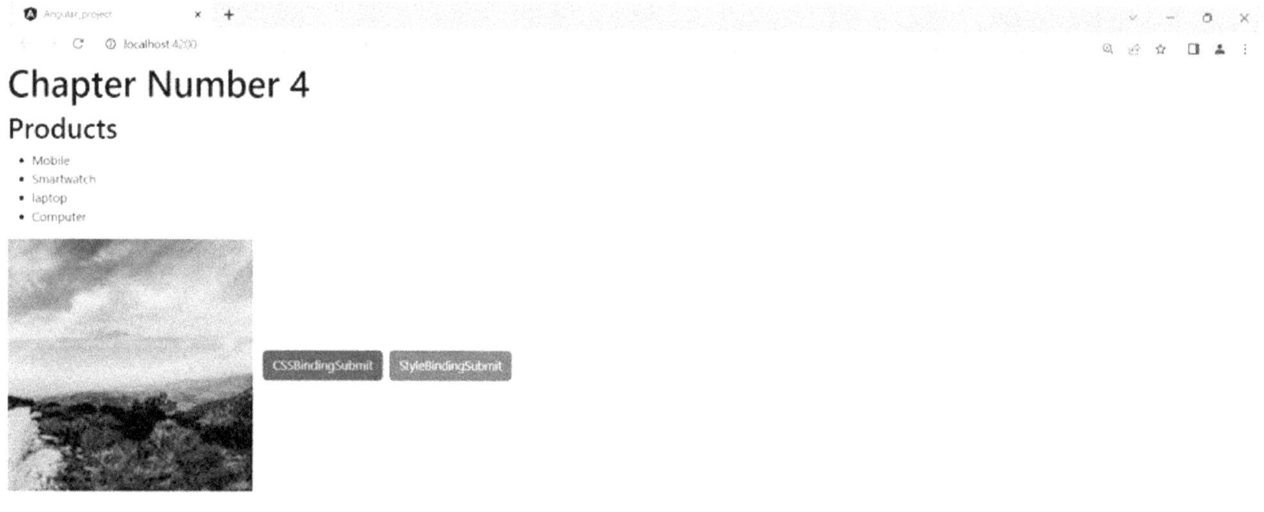

4.4 Event Binding

We use event binding to handle events raised by the DOM like clicks, mouse movements, key strokes and so on. When you are clicking on buttons or mouse clicks will be there or mouse cursors has been moved. Similar to property binding, we have two syntaxes for event binding. parenthesis () or prefix.

In your component you can have template just like button class where we have used here you can also have separate buttons. For example, we initially used it as class.active and save it then multiple buttons will get displayed. So in browser we see two buttons as submit submit it is active then it is darker in shade and we used style binding for second button. If it is false then first button will lighter in shade and second button will be with gray background.

We have click events on the button so for that we will add one more button and label to it. So first button was our CSSBinding these is our style binding button and we will be creating it for click event so for these again in these button we will use two different syntaxes first with parenthesis. So we can have onClick event in double quotes as click event will passing here.

```
@Component({
selector: 'app-root',
template: `
<button (click)="onClick($event)">EventBindingSubmit</button>
`

})
export class AppComponent {
```

```
onClick($event){
console.log("Clicked",$event)
}
}
```

In the above code, we illustrate event binding using parenthesis. We put the target event name (click) name in the parenthesis and then assign it to the onClick($event) method in our component.

Alternatively, we can also have,

<button on-click="onClick($event)">Submit</button> where we add the prefix on- before the target event.

When the button is clicked, the onClick method is called. The $event argument in onClick($event) allows us to get access to the event raised. For example, in mouse movements, the event object will tell us the x and y position. We can also use the event object to get access to the DOM element that raised the event. Note that there is a $ prefix in $event because this is built into Angular. The event object is a standard DOM event object and has got nothing to do with Angular.

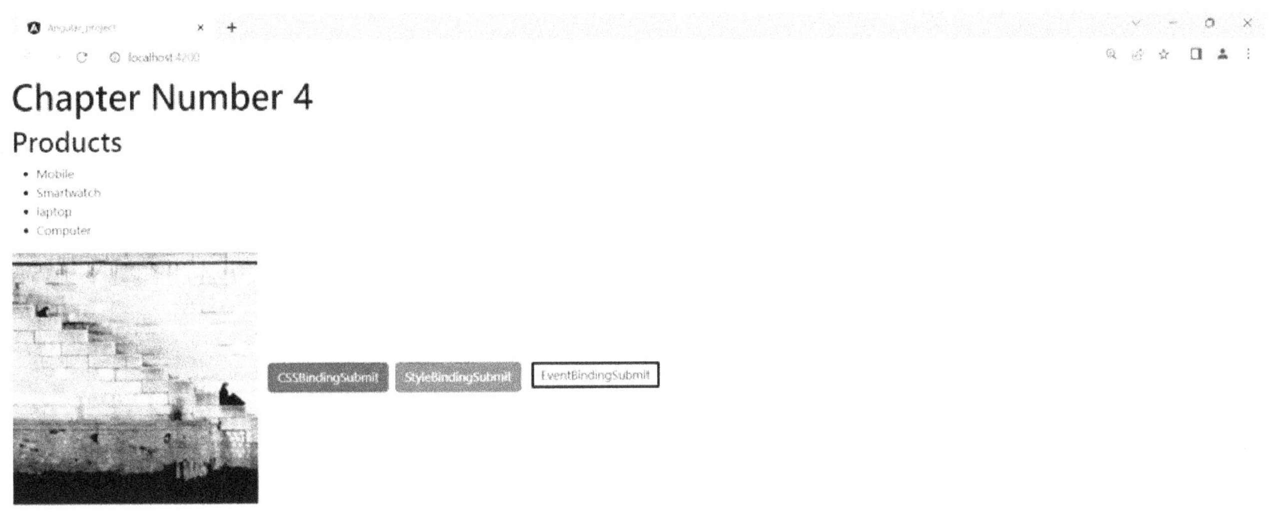

4.5 Two-way Binding

In two-way binding the communication will be at both the end so that means whenever we make any changes in DOM element then it will get reflected back in component. In Angular, there is a directive called ngModel to create two-way binding between a component property and a DOM property in the view. Remember that a directive is a class that allows us to control or extend the behaviour of a DOM. We illustrate two-way binding using ngModel in the below code.

```
@Component({
selector: 'app-root',
template: `
<input type="text" [(ngModel)]="title"/>
You have typed: {{title}}
`
})
export class AppComponent {
}
```

In this code, we take an example DOM element as text field for that purpose we can have input with type attribute as text so we will have text box. Along with that we will be using ngModel directive and this is inside in the input tag and whatever will be typed inside this text box should get displayed. When you run the app, whatever you type in the input field is displayed in the DOM as well.

In the input field, we add [(ngModel)]="title" to bind our DOM input property to the component's title property. But realize that the component property is also bind to the DOM in the code You have typed: {{title}}

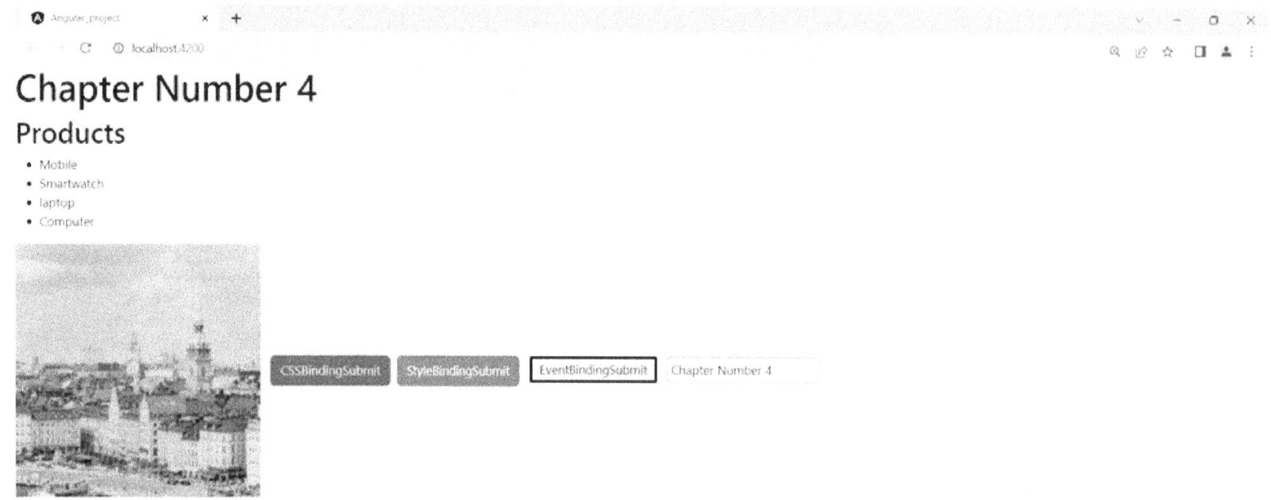

4.6 Example Application

Now we will see an example in which data binding will build as you know rating component.

These ratings are provided by using stars. Just for example as in applications e.g Amazon or Flipkart. We can implement this as a component and reuse it in many places. A user can click select from a rating of one star to five stars. For now, we will not interest in server or any other logic. We just want to implement the user interface (UI).

Open the existing project folder from chapter two, create a new component class rating.component.ts and fill it with the below code.

rating.component.ts

```
import { Component } from '@angular/core'
@Component({
selector: 'rating',
template: `
<i
class="glyphicon"
[class.glyphicon-star-empty]="rating<1"
[class.glyphicon-star]="rating>=1"
(click)="onClick(1)"
>
</i>
`

})
export class RatingComponent{
```

```
rating = 0;
onClick(ratingValue){
this.rating = ratingValue;
}
}
```

In this code import component using decorator component and inside that we will having selector and template. The style will be using for selector is rating because we are creating the rating component so we'll be using rating tag then we will having template for it here backtick is used we will having a class as glyphicon also having class.glyphicon with empty star.

If rating is less than 1 and it will be filled 1 if rating is greater than or equals to 1. Now the class.glyphicon with star if greater than or equals to 1 and it should be taken for click event and closed the tag. We will export the rating component here, we will be taking rating initially as zero and when user click on it so it should be having rating value here. It should get assigned with the rating variable so one value will be assigned to it.

Next in app.module.ts, import the rating component and add it to the declarations array by adding the below lines in **bold**. By adding RatingComponent to declarations , we specify that it is part of AppModule and can therefore be used in AppComponent.

app.module.ts

```
import { ProductsComponent } from './products.component';
import { RatingComponent } from './rating.component';
import { ProductService } from './product.service';
@NgModule({
declarations: [ AppComponent, ProductsComponent, RatingComponent ],
imports: [ BrowserModule, FormsModule, HttpModule, ],
//providers: [ProductService],
providers: [],
bootstrap: [AppComponent]
})
export class AppModule { }
```

Lastly, in app.component.ts , add the < rating> element in the template as shown below:

```
import { Component } from '@angular/core';
@Component({
selector: 'app-root',
template: `
<rating></rating>
`

})
export class AppComponent {
}
```

Code Explanation:

```
@Component({
selector: 'rating',
template: `
<i
class="glyphicon"
[class.glyphicon-star-empty]="rating<1"
[class.glyphicon-star]="rating>=1"
(click)="onClick(1)"
>
```

```
</i>
`
})
```

We define a component called Rating Component with selector as 'rating' so in app.component.ts , we create an instance of it with **<rating></rating>** .

In the template, we render bootstrap glyphicons using class="glyphicon" and use class binding to conditionally render a secondary class with

```
[class.glyphicon-star-empty]="rating < 1"
[class.glyphicon-star]="rating >= 1"
```

The condition is based on the property rating defined in the RatingComponent class below.

```
export class RatingComponent{
rating = 0;
onClick(ratingValue){
this.rating = ratingValue;
}
}
```

The condition works like the following, if the rating is less than one, we render the empty star icon.

```
[class.glyphicon-star-empty]="rating < 1"
```

If the rating is more than or equal to one, we render the normal star icon.

```
[class.glyphicon-star]="rating >= 1"
```

We add a click handler (click)="onClick(1)" to assign a rating of one if a user clicks on this star.

You would probably notice that we have only one star at this point of time, when ratings usually have five stars. This is because I wanted you to be familiar with the logic of one star. To then extend it to five stars is easy. Simply copy and paste the glyphicon code in the template for additional stars as shown below.

```
@Component({
selector: 'rating',
template: `
<i
class="glyphicon"
[class.glyphicon-star-empty]="rating<1"
[class.glyphicon-star]="rating>=1"
(click)="onClick(1)"
>
</i>
<i
class="glyphicon"
[class.glyphicon-star-empty]="rating<2"
[class.glyphicon-star]="rating>=2"
(click)="onClick(2)"
>
</i>
<i
class="glyphicon"
[class.glyphicon-star-empty]="rating<3"
[class.glyphicon-star]="rating>=3"
(click)="onClick(3)"
>
</i>
```

```
<i
class="glyphicon"
[class.glyphicon-star-empty]="rating<4"
[class.glyphicon-star]="rating>=4"
(click)="onClick(4)"
>
</i>
<i
class="glyphicon"
[class.glyphicon-star-empty]="rating<5"
[class.glyphicon-star]="rating>=5"
(click)="onClick(5)"
>
</i>
`
})
```

Note that you need to do two things. Firstly, change the value of each condition depending on which star it is. The second star's condition should be

```
[class.glyphicon-star-empty]="rating < 2"
[class.glyphicon-star]="rating >= 2"
```

The second star should be empty if the rating is less than two. It should be filled if the rating is more than or equal to two. The same goes for the third, fourth and fifth star.

Secondly, change the value of the argument when you called the onClick method depending on which star it is. The second star's onClick should be (click)="onClick(2)" . So when a user clicks on the second star, the onClick method is called with property rating of value two. When a user clicks on the third star, the onClick method is called with property rating of value three and so on and lastly our output look like

CHAPTER FIVE

Building Reusable Components

Angular & TypeScript Building Reusable Components, Component Input Properties, Component Output Properties, Templates, Styles, API, Displaying Multiple Products with Product Image, Name, Date, Rating, Number of Reviews, Description

In this chapter we will learn about How to build reusable components. So till now we have create two components product & rating components. In this chapter learn about component and how to reused in a application.

A Reusable component is a piece of User Interface that can be used in many parts of an application to build and render different User Interface instances.

5.1 Component Input Properties

Component properties can be input properties & output properties. So input & output properties that can consider as a public API for the component. So properties marks as input or output Visible in property binding or event binding

For ex:-

<button [value]="title"(click)= "onclick($event)" > submit </button>

In this example value is a example of input property. Click event is bind to the method onclick & onclick method you can define inside component class click is the example of output property. Here input & output Property has be define the button element, So the input & output from the API of button. you can also define a public API (Application public Interface) for custom component user define component. just for ex., we have learn about previous chapter rating components if you want to display list of products with product Image, name ,date ,rating number of reviews & description.

5.2 Template

In Angular template is a part of HTML use special syntax within template to create many of Angular Features each angular template in your application is a chunk of HTML to be include as Part of the page displayed by the browser. An angular HTML template renders a view or user interface , in the browser like regular HTML but with much more functionality.

When you generate an Angular application with the angular CLI the app.component.html file is the default template containing the placeholder HTML.

Basically we are seen our rating component we have created a template for a rating whenever rating tag will be occurring so this template used for the rating component thin template inside the component itself so template code is small then better to define our component but if it is large in size then we should write a template in inline in the component we can have separated template file just for ex, for **rating.component.ts** we can create app folder a new file just for example rating.component.html we can create this separate file & complete template code copy from **rating.component.ts** an that can be pasted in inside the rating.component.html file. In **rating.component.ts** component part we write 'templateUrl' : rating.component.html

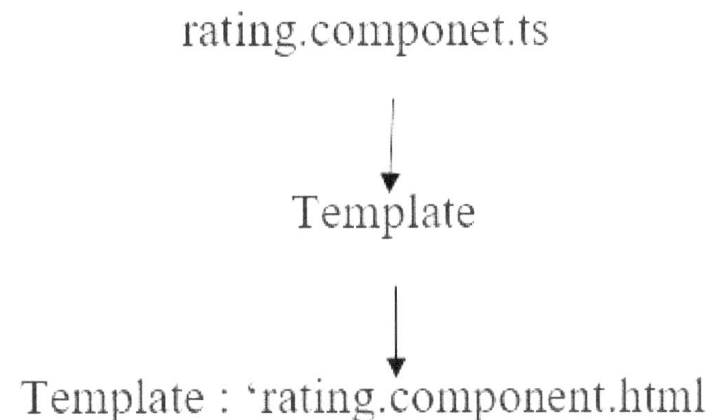

5.3 Styles

Angular application are styled with standard CSS. That mean's with you can everything you know about CSS. Stylesheets , selectors ,rules and media queries directly to angular application. Another useful component meta data is styles just like your template you can have styles: or StyleUrls :

Another useful field in the component metadata is styles or styleUrls . Similar to template , you can define css styles required by your component in the styles array or in a separate file(s) with styleUrls . A notable feature is that these styles are scoped to your component. They won't effect to the outer html or other components. To illustrate, suppose we want our filled glyphicon stars to be orange, we add the following in bold.

When we run our application, we will see our filled stars with the orange css applied to it.

Rating.component.ts :-

Inside the rating.component.ts we will added the style code We can applied various element it is an array inside multiple element & here bactic sige we want to applied to glyphicon-star inside start property we used orange color

```
import { Component,Input} from "@angular/core";
@Component({
selector:'rating',
templateUrl:`rating.component.html`,
styles:[`
.glyphicon-star{
Color : orange;
}`]
})
export class RatingComponent
{
//rating=0;
@Input() rating=0;
@Input() numOfReviews=0;
onClick(ratingValue:number){
this.rating=ratingValue;
}
}
```

Instead of having our html in template , we specify the url to our template file in templateUrl . At the risk of sounding obvious, do note that youcannot use both template and templateUrl at the same time.

5.4 Reuse Rating Cpmponents

Reuse the rating component from displaying the product listing so we can have multiple products an their will be rating in front of it display 5 star filed or unfiled so this product list is the finding of e-commers application such as amazon , flipkart , Zomato etc. basically list of the product we will try to create product image , product name if you observed on amazon or flipkart what thinks has been display so product image , product name , date of the product , rating of that product.

product.component.ts :-

We are created the new file product.component.ts for the new product listing. So now Again import the component & input from the '@angular/core' we are add the @component , this are acting as a function, component we have selector 'product' then having template ,and creating a style inside the div tag style will be apply for product listing properly formatted. Then define the class here so export class name it as product components so here we used input property. Inside the template we are added the media class.go to the google search the getbootstrap media object so media object there are two part layout or component so we select the component and copy the media heading then pest to our template.

```
import {Component, Input} from '@angular/core'
@Component ({
selector:'product',
template:`
<div class="media">
<img src="{{data.imageUrl}}" class="media-object" alt="...">
<div class="media-body">
<h4 class="media-heading">
{{data.productName}}
</h4>
{{data.releasedDate }}
<rating
[rating]="data.rating"
[numOfReviews]="data.numofReviews">
</rating>
<br>
{{data.description }}
</div>
</div>
</div>
`,
styles:[`
.media{
margin-bottom:20px;
}`]
})
export class ProductComponent {
@Input() data;
}
```

Inside the code we include the data. Data will be include imageurl , productName, releasedDate & description this are the input filed rating component rating input from the data object numOfReviews.

Next we are create the new file product.service.ts

product.service.ts:-

Next, we create a new file product.service.ts that contains a service class ProductService that is responsible for returning a list of products. Type in the below code into ProductService class.

Inside the product service class having the method 'getProducts()' inside this method I will return imageUrl , productName , releasedDate , description & rating numofReviews

```
export class ProductService{
getProucts(){
return[
{
imageUrl:"https://loremflickr.com/150/150?random=1" ,
productName:"Product 1",
//releasedDate:"May 29,2020",
releasedDate: new Date(2003,5,27), //"May 29,2020",
description:"This is product 1",
rating:4,
numOfReviews:3
},
{
imageUrl:"https://loremflickr.com/150/150?random=2" ,
productName:"Product 2",
releasedDate:"March 30,2021",
description:"This is product 2",
rating:2,
numOfReviews:30
},
{
imageUrl:"https://loremflickr.com/150/150?random=3" ,
productName:"Product 3",
releasedDate:"August 30,2022",
description:"This is product 3",
rating:5,
numOfReviews:8
}];
}
}
```

Fill all details in product , here I can sign any image so search the loremflickr.com use any image path & select size.

Products.component.ts:-

getproduct () function I will call it inside the products.component.ts

```
import{Component} from '@angular/core'
import { ProductService } from './product.service';
@Component({
selector:'products',
template:`
<h2>Product</h2>
```

```
<div *ngIf="products.length>0">
<div *ngFor = "let product of products">
<product [data]="product"></product>
</div>
</div>
<div *ngIf="products.length==0">
No Products to Display
</div>
`,
providers:[ProductService]
})
export class ProductsComponent
{
products;
constructor(productService: ProductService){
this.products = productService.getProucts();
}
}
```

The ngFor loops through products array as retrieved from ProductService and inputs each data element in the products array for each product component. Each data element provides Product component with values from properties imageUrl, productName, releasedData and description. We also import ProductService and declare it in the providers array to specify that we depend on ProductService as a service provider. Lastly in app.module.ts in the lines in below, we import ProductComponent and add it to the declarations array to declare ProductComponent as part of AppModule.

```
import { BrowserModule } from '@angular/platform-browser';
import { NgModule } from '@angular/core';
import { FormsModule } from '@angular/forms';
import { HttpModule } from '@angular/http';
import { AppComponent } from './app.component';
import { ProductsComponent } from './products.component';
import { ProductComponent } from './product.component';
import { RatingComponent } from './rating.component';
import { ProductService } from './product.service';
@NgModule({
declarations: [
AppComponent, ProductsComponent, RatingComponent, ProductComponent
],
imports: [
BrowserModule,
FormsModule,
HttpModule,
],
providers: [],
bootstrap: [AppComponent]
})
export class AppModule { }
```

In this chapter, we illustrate how to define input properties in a component, use both inline templates and templates defined in a separate file with templateUrl , use styles to define css styles used in a component and borrow markup from bootstrap to put all these together in our example Product Listing application

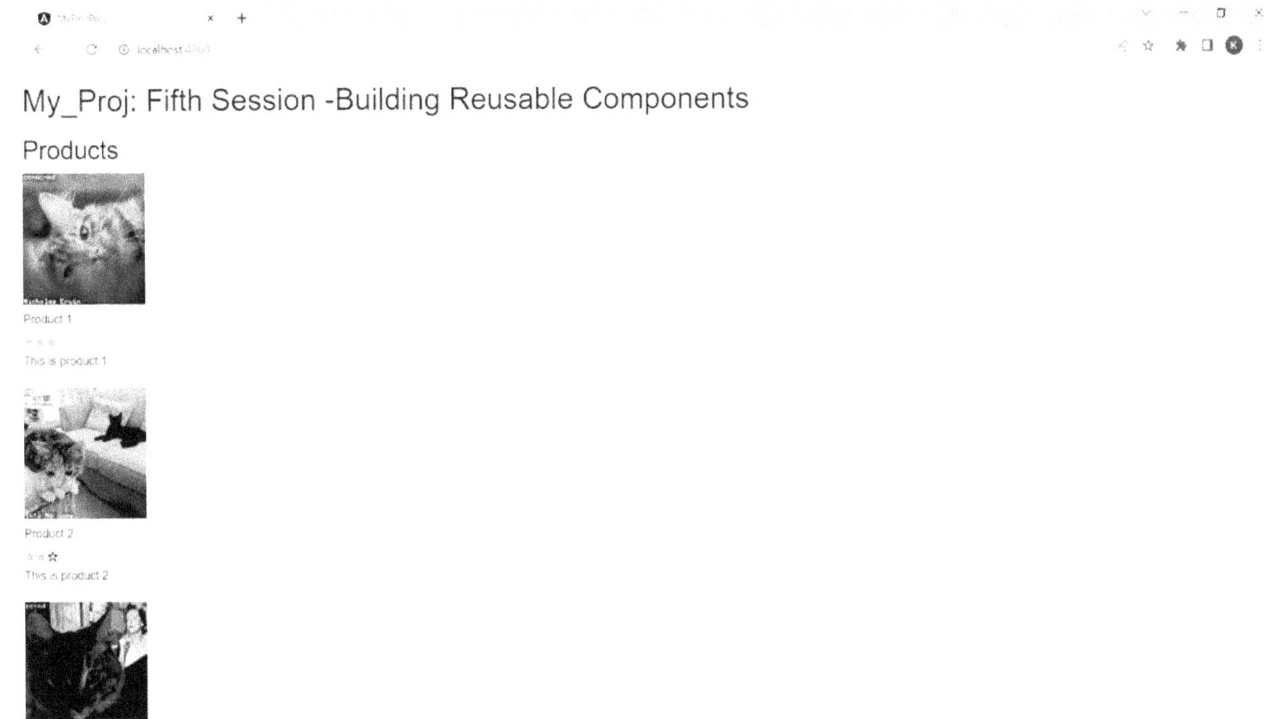

CHAPTER SIX

Controlling Rendering of HTML

We have worked with ngFor which is one of the built in directives in Angular. In this chapter, we will explore more built-in directives which will give us more control in rendering html.

6.1 ngIf

Suppose you want to show or hide part of a view depending on some condition. For example, we have earlier displayed our list of products. But if there are no products to display, we want to display a message like "No products to display" on the page.

products.component.ts

```
import { Component } from '@angular/core'
import { ProductService} from './product.service'
@Component({
selector: 'products',
template: `
<h2>Products</h2>
<div *ngIf="products.length > 0">
<div *ngFor="let product of products">
<product [data]="product"></product>
</div>
</div>
<div *ngIf="products.length == 0">
No products to display
</div>
`,
providers: [ProductService]
})
export class ProductsComponent{
products;
constructor(productService: ProductService){
this.products = productService.getProducts();
}
}
```

Now when we run our app again, we should see the products displayed as same as before. But if we comment out our hard-coded data in ProductService and return an empty array instead, we should get the following message.

Products

No products to display

Code Explanation

```
<div *ngIf="products.length > 0">
<div *ngFor="let product of products">
<product [data]="product"></product>
</div>
</div>
```

We used the *ngIf directive to add a i f- condition in our DOM and assign an expression “ ***products.length*** *>* ***0*** ” to it. If the expression evaluates to true, the div element and its children will be inserted into the DOM. If it evaluates to false, it will be removed from the DOM. When there are products returned from ProductService , the expression evaluates to true and renders the products in the ngFor loop.

The following expression however evaluates to false and therefore, we don’t display the message.

```
<div *ngIf="products.length == 0">
No products to display
</div>
```

When we return an empty array however, “ ***products.length*** *>* ***0*** ” evaluates to false and we do not render the list of products. Instead, we display the “No products to display message”.

6.2 ngSwitch

In a similar fashion as ngIf, the ngSwitch statement allows us to render elements and its children based on a condition against a list of values. Suppose we want to add a comment based on the product rating

where one star means 'Poor', two star - 'Fair', three star - Good, four star - 'Very Good', five star - 'Excellent'. We can achieve this by adding the below code in **bold** into the template fieldof ***product.component.ts*** .

```
template: `
<div class="media">
<div class="media-left">
<a href="#">
<img class="media-object" src="{{ data.imageUrl }}">
</a>
</div>
<div class="media-body">
<h4 class="media-heading">
{{ data.productName }}
</h4>
{{ data.releasedDate }}
```

```
<rating
[rating-value]="data.rating"
[numOfReviews]="data.numOfReviews">
</rating>
<div [ngSwitch]="data.rating">
<div *ngSwitchCase="1">Poor</div>
<div *ngSwitchCase="2">Fair</div>
<div *ngSwitchCase="3">Good</div>
<div *ngSwitchCase="4">Very Good</div>
<div *ngSwitchCase="5">Excellent</div>
<div *ngSwitchDefault>Not Rated</div>
</div>
<br>
{{ data.description }}
</div>
</div>
`,
```

So depending on the value of data.rating , we display different product comments. We use *ngSwitchDefault in the case where the value of data.rating does not match any of the cases, we display a default message 'Not Rated'.

6.3 Pipes

To format data in Angular, we can use 'pipes. A pipe takes in data as input and transforms it to a desired output. Angular has built in pipes like DatePipe , UpperCasePipe , LowerCasePipe , CurrencyPipe , and PercentPipe . We can also create custom pipes which we will visit in the next section. Because pipes are relatively straightforward, we will illustrate the DatePipe and you can go on to explore the rest of the built in pipes on your own.

First, we change the value of releasedDate in the object returned by ProductService to a Javascript Date object as shown in bold below.

```
return [
{
imageUrl: "http://loremflickr.com/150/150?random=1",
productName: "Product 1",
releasedDate: new Date(2016,5,30),
description: "...",
rating: 4,
numOfReviews: 2
},
```

We have assigned releasedDate with a Date object with value 30 Jun, 2016. (Note that the month count starts from 0). Now, the date gets displayed as " Thu Jun 30 2016 00:00:00 GMT+0800 (SGT) " which is not what we want to display to the user. To use pipe formating, in product.component.ts , we do the below,

```
{{ data.releasedDate | date }}
```

The date now gets displayed as Jun 30, 2016.

Parameterizing a Pipe

We can also supply pipes with optional parameters to fine tune its format. We do so by adding a colon (:) and then the parameter value (e.g., date:"MM/dd/yy"). The below code returns our date 06/30/16 in the specified format of MM/dd/yy.

```
{{ data.releasedDate | date:"MM/dd/yy" }} // 06/30/16
```

Chaining Pipes

We can also chain pipes together for useful combinations. In the below example, we chain releasedDate to DatePipe and on to UpperCasePipe to display the date in uppercase. The following birthday displays as JUN 30, 2016.

{{ data.releasedDate | date | uppercase }} // JUN 30, 2016

6.4 Custom Pipes

We can also write our own custom pipes. We use custom pipes the same way we use built-in pipes. We will implement a custom pipe that takes a string and truncate it to a specified length. This is useful for displaying a truncated product description in the view if it is too long like

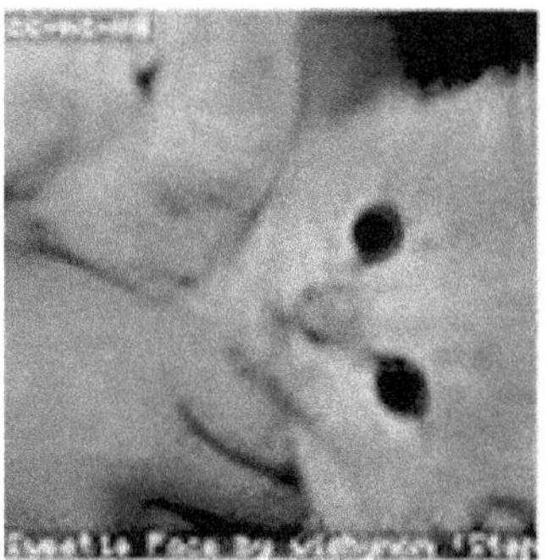

First, create a new file ***truncate.pipe.ts*** in the app folder. Type in the below codes into the file.

truncate.pipe.ts

```
import { Pipe, PipeTransform } from '@angular/core';
@Pipe({name: 'truncate'})
```

```
export class TruncatePipe implements PipeTransform {
transform(value: string, limit:number): string{
return value.substring(0,limit) + "...";
}
}
```

Code Explanation

A pipe is a plain TypeScript class decorated with pipe metadata ***@Pipe({name:'truncate'})*** . We tell Angular this is a pipe by applying the @Pipe decorator which we import from the core Angular library. The @Pipe decorator allows us to define the pipe name that we'll use within template expressions. Our pipe's name is truncate.

Every pipe class implements the PipeTransform interface's transform method. The transform method accepts an input value followed by optional parameters and returns the transformed value. In our code, value is the string we want to truncate and limit determines the limit of our truncation.

```
export class TruncatePipe implements PipeTransform {
transform(value: string, limit:number): string{
return value.substring(0,limit) + "...";
}
}
```

Final Steps

Next, we have to include our pipe in the declarations array of the AppModule to specify that our pipe is part of the AppModule. Add the lines below in **bold** to ***app.module.ts*** .

```
import { BrowserModule } from '@angular/platform-browser';
...
...
import { RatingComponent } from './rating.component';
import { TruncatePipe } from './truncate.pipe';
@NgModule({
declarations: [
AppComponent, ProductsComponent, RatingComponent, ProductComponent, TruncatePipe
],
imports: [
...
],
providers: [],
bootstrap: [AppComponent]
})
export class AppModule { }
```

Finally in ***product.component.ts*** , add the pipe to the data.description interpolation like,

{{ data.description | truncate: 20}}

6.5 ng-content

Sometimes, we need to insert content into our component from the outside. For example, we want to implement a component that wraps a bootstrap jumbotron. A bootstrap jumbotron (fig. 5.6.1) as defined on getbootstrap.com is "A lightweight, flexible component that can optionally extend the entire viewport to showcase key content on your site."

Here is an implementation of the bootstrap jumbotron component.

```
import { Component, Input } from '@angular/core';
@Component({
selector: 'bs-jumbotron',
template: `
<div class="jumbotron">
<p></p>
<p><a class="btn btn-primary btn-lg" href="#" role="button"></a></p>
</div>
`
})
export class JumboTronComponent {
}
```

The markup above can be obtained from http://getbootstrap.com/components/#jumbotron.

The selector is bs-jumbotron . We add a prefix bs- ('bs' as an abbreviation for bootstrap) to distinguish this component from other components that potentially might have the same name. The jumbotron component is called in ***app.component.ts*** using,

```
import { Component } from '@angular/core';
@Component({
selector: 'app-root',
template: `
<bs-jumbotron></bs-jumbotron>
`
})
export class AppComponent {
}
```

To supply content to the jumbotron component, we can use Input properties. We can define an Input property in our jumbotron component and use property binding as shown below:

```
<bs-jumbotron [body]="..."></bs-jumbotron>
```

This is not ideal however. For we probably want to write a lengthier html markup here like,

```
<bs-jumbotron>
This is a simple hero unit, a simple jumbotron-style component for calling extra attention to featured content or information.
</bs-jumbotron>
```

We want to insert content into the jumbotron component from the outside. To do so, we define insertion points with ng-content as shown below into our jumbotron component template.

```
@Component({
selector: 'bs-jumbotron',
template: `
<div class="jumbotron">
<p><ng-content></ng-content></p>
<p><a class="btn btn-primary btn-lg" href="#" role="button"></a></p>
</div>
`
})
export class JumboTronComponent {
}
```

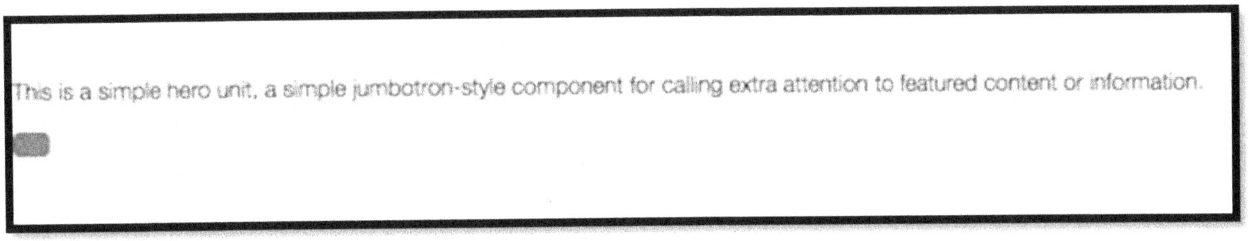

This is a simple hero unit, a simple jumbotron-style component for calling extra attention to featured content or information.

Multiple Insertion Points

We can also define multiple insertion points by adding the select directive. In ***bsjumbotron.component.ts*** , we do this by using ng-content and specifying a css class to the select attribute to distinguish where content should go.

```
import { Component, Input } from '@angular/core';
@Component({
selector: 'bs-jumbotron',
template: `
<div class="jumbotron">
<h1><ng-content select=".heading"></ng-content></h1>
<p><ng-content select=".body"></ng-content></p>
<p><a class="btn btn-primary btn-lg" href="#" role="button">
<ng-content select=".button"></ng-content></a></p>
</div>
`
})
export class JumboTronComponent {
}
```

In the above code, we specify that content with the class heading will be placed in the h1 heading tag. Content with class body will be placed in the body and content with class button will be in the button.

We now add in ***app.component.ts*** the rest of the text with the various css classes as shown below.

```
@Component({
```

```
selector: 'app-root',
template: `
<bs-jumbotron>
<div class="heading">
Hello World!
</div>
<div class="body">
This is a simple hero unit, a simple jumbotron-style component for calling extra
attention to featured content or information.
</div>
<div class="button">
Learn more
</div>
</bs-jumbotron>
`
})
export class AppComponent {
}
```

If you run your app now, you should now see something like in figure

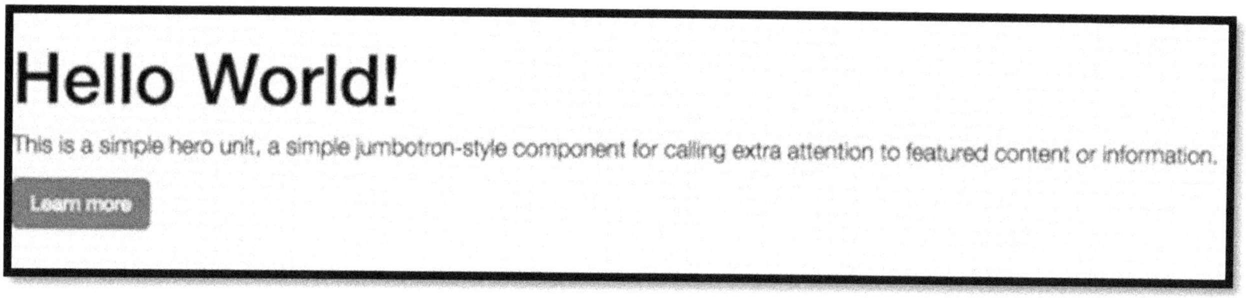

Hello World!

This is a simple hero unit, a simple jumbotron-style component for calling extra attention to featured content or information.

Learn more

CHAPTER SEVEN

Template Driven Forms

In Angular there are two types of Forms model driven forms and template driven forms. In this chapter we will discus template driven forms. Template driven forms are easier to implement and involve writing less code. But they give us limited control over validation. Model driven forms have more code but we have full control over validation.

So initial for design template driven form will create the USER model class. We create our form, we want to define a class or model that can hold the data that we receive from the form. A model is represented by a simple class that contains properties. We will create a User class with two required fields (first name, email) and one optional field (country).

7.1 Create the User Model Class

Firstly we create the user.ts file inside the app folder then we define a class User, constructor having three field first-name, email & country. First-name ang email field are required field and country field are optional field.

```
export class User {
constructor(
public firstName: string,
public email: string,
public country?: string
) { }
}
```

Now next we create the user-form.component.ts file inside the app folder inside the user-form component.ts again we import the component from core angular module and import the User class from User In the UserFormComponent. We import the User model we just created. We specify our selector to be user-form. Because the html markup will be quite long, we use the templateUrl property to point to a separate html file user-form.component.html for our template.

```
import { Component } from '@angular/core';
import { User } from './user';
@Component({
selector: 'user-form',
templateUrl: 'user-form.component.html'
})
export class UserFormComponent {
countries = ['United States', 'Singapore', 'Hong Kong', 'Australia'];
model = new User('','','');
submitted = false;
onSubmit() {
this.submitted = true;
}
}
```

7.2 Create HTML Form Template

Template-driven form features are in FormsModule, we need to add it to the imports array in app.module.ts if we have not already done so. FormsModule gives our application access to template-driven forms features, including ngModel. We also import the UserFormComponent and add it to declarations array in app.module.ts so that UserFormComponent is accessible throughout this module.

In app.module.ts we already import the FormModule similarly we have import the UserFormComponent and we added in the declaration also.

Next, create our template file user-form.component.html inside the app folder

```
<div class="container">
<h1>User Form</h1>
<form>
<div class="form-group">
<label for="firstName">First Name</label>
<input type="text" class="form-control" id="firstName" required>
</div>
<div class="form-group">
<label for="email">Email</label>
<input type="text" class="form-control" id="email" required>
</div>
<div class="form-group">
<label for="country">Country</label>
<input type="text" class="form-control" id="country">
<select class="form-control" id="country">
<option *ngFor="let c of countries" [value]="c">{{c}}</option>
</select>
</div>
<button type="submit" class="btn btn-default">Submit</button>
</form>
</div>
```

Our form definition till now is just plain html. We are not using Angular yet. We allow firstName and email fields for user input in input boxes. Both firstName and email has the html required attribute; the country does not have required because it is optional. At the end we have a Submit button.

In the country field, we choose one country from a fixed list of countries using select dropdown. We will retrieve the list of countries from an array in UserFormComponent and bind the options to the country list using ngFor.

With *ngFor , we repeat the tag for each country in the list of countries. The variable c holds a different country element in each iteration and we display it using interpolation {{c}}.

7.3 Two-way data binding with ngModel

Two-way data binding for that purpose we used mgModel , create two way binding between our form and the User model.

Now Update the firstname,

```
<div class="form-group">
<label for="firstName">First Name</label>
<input type="text" class="form-control" id="firstName" required
[(ngModel)]="model.firstName" name="firstName">
```

```
</div>
```

We have also added a name attribute to our tag and set it to firstName. We can assign any unique value, but we should use a descriptive name like the name of the input. The name attribute is required by Angular Forms to register the control with the form. Do the same for the rest of the fields as in below.

```
<div class="container">
<h1>User Form</h1>
<form>
<div class="form-group">
<label for="firstName">First Name</label>
<input type="text" class="form-control" id="firstName" required
[(ngModel)]="model.firstName" name="firstName">
</div>
<div class="form-group">
<label for="email">Email</label>
<input type="text" class="form-control" id="email" required
[(ngModel)]="model.email" name="email">
</div>
<div class="form-group">
<label for="country">Country</label>
<select class="form-control" id="country"
[(ngModel)]="model.country" name="country">
<option *ngFor="let c of countries" [value]="c">{{c}}</option>
</select>
</div>
<button type="submit" class="btn btn-default">Submit</button>
</form>
</div>
```

That the id property in each input or select is used by the label to match to its for attribute so that when a user clicks on the label, the input or select receives the focus therefore enabling better user interaction since a user can either click on the label or input itself for the right focus.

Inside app.component.ts added the à <user-form></user-form>

7.4 Track change-state and validity with ngModel

ngModel not only provide us with two way data binding between the form and controls, it also allows us to track change state and validity of the controls. This is useful to let us know if an input has been filled in and if the input is valid so that we can display alert or warning messages to the user. For a control with ngModel directive, if a user has touched the control, the control's Angular css class ng-touched returns true and ng-untouched returns false. The reverse is true. If the value of the control is changed, its ng-dirty class returns true and ngpristine returns false. The reverse is true. If the value of the control is valid, ng-valid class returns true and ng-invalid returns false. The reverse is true.

In the below code, we firstly add the #firstName variable and give it the value ngModel to create a reference to the firstName input control so that we can access its css classes. Next, we show the " First Name is required " message if firstName.touched is true and firstName.valid is false. Note that we have divided the markup of the input element into multiple lines instead of one single line so that it is easier to see its attributes.

```
<div class="form-group">
<label for="firstName">First Name</label>
<input type="text" class="form-control" id="firstName" required
```

```
[(ngModel)]="model.firstName" name="firstName"
#firstName="ngModel" >
<div class="alert alert-danger"
*ngIf="firstName.touched && !firstName.valid ">
First name is required
</div>
</div>
```

Why do we check touched? This is to avoid showing errors before the user has had a chance to edit the value, for example when the form is freshly loaded. This prevents premature display of errors. We proceed to do the same for email input.

```
<div class="form-group">
<label for="email">Email</label>
<input type="text" class="form-control" id="email" required
[(ngModel)]="model.email" name="email" #email="ngModel">
<div *ngIf="email.touched && !email.valid"
Class="alert alert-danger">Email is required.
</div>
</div>
```

7.5 Showing Specific Validation Errors

Other than the required validation, we can also specify our input validation on an element's minimum and maximum length using its minlength and maxlength html validation attributes. The below code illustrates this.

```
<div *ngIf="firstName.touched && firstName.errors">
<div class="alert alert-danger"
*ngIf="firstName.errors.required">
First name is required
</div>
<div class="alert alert-danger"
*ngIf="firstName.errors.minlength">
First name should be minimum 3 characters.
</div>
</div>
```

The first *ngIf on the outer element reveals two nested message divs if the control is touched and there are firstName errors. Inside the outer are two nested which presents a custom message for required and minlength validation error.

7.6 Submit the form with ngSubmit

To implement submitting of forms, we update theTop of Form tag with the Angular directive NgSubmit and bind it to the UserFormComponent.submit() method with an event binding in the below code.

```
<form (ngSubmit)="onSubmit()" #userForm="ngForm">
```

In the Top of Formtag, we also define a variable #userForm and assign the value "ngForm" to it to make userForm a reference to the form as a whole. The ngForm directive allows userForm to hold control to its contained elements with the ngModel directive and name attribute. userForm thus allows us to monitor these contained control elements' properties including their validity. userForm also has its own valid property which is true only if every contained control is valid. This enables us tobind the Submit button's disabled property to the form's over-all validity via the #userForm variable. That is, the Submit button remains disabled until all required inputs are filled up properly. We do this with the below code in the Submit button.

```
<button type="submit" class="btn btn-default"
[disabled]="!userForm.form.valid">Submit</button>
```

7.7 Getting Submitted Values

To show that we have successfully submitted our form with its values, add the below code to the bottom of user-form.component.html.

```
<div [hidden]="!submitted">
You submitted the following:
First Name: {{ model.firstName }}<br>
Email: {{ model.email }}<br>
Country: {{ model.country }}<br>
<button class="btn btn-default"
(click)="submitted=false">Remove</button>
</div>
```

In this chapter, we learnt how to create a template driven form. We created a model class to represent the data in the form, used *ngFor to display the list of options in a select dropdown, created two-way binding with form and component properties using ngModel , used ngModel to help us show form field validation errors, and finally learnt form submission using ngSubmit.

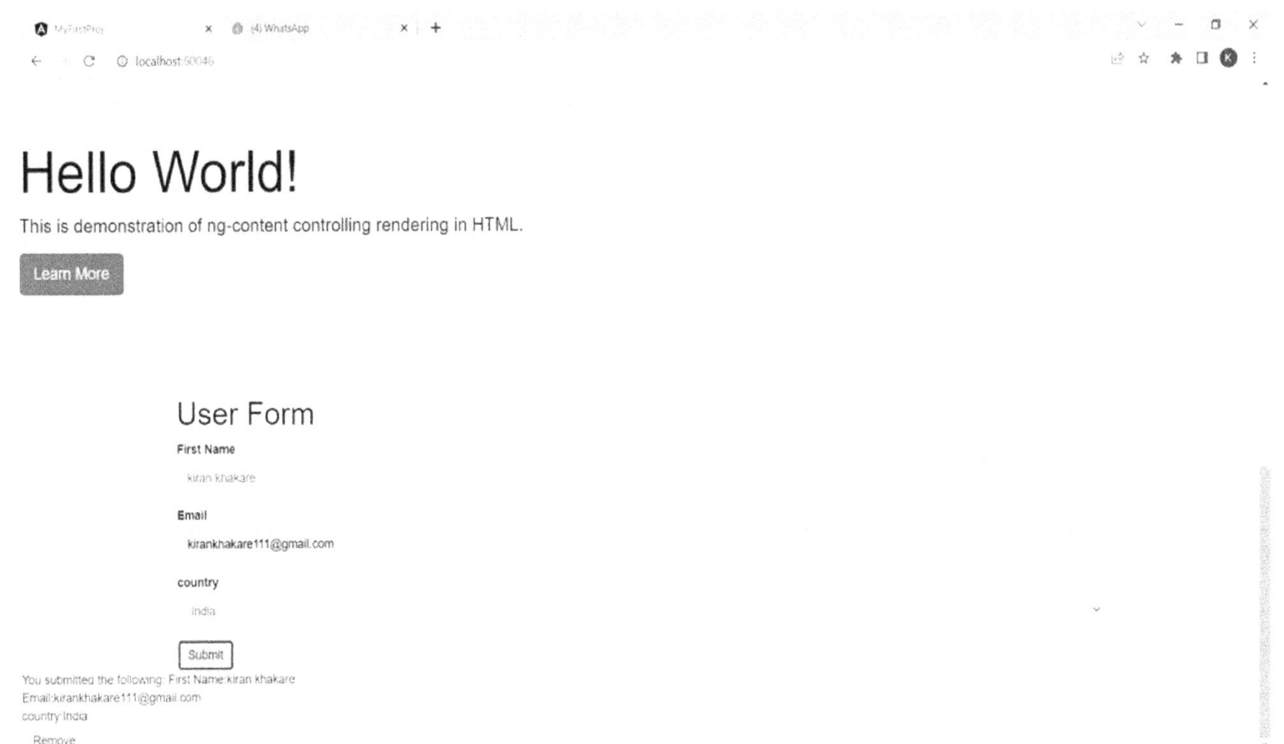

CHAPTER EIGHT

Model Driven Forms

In this chapter we will see the Model Driven Forms. In previous chapter we are learn about Template Driven Forms, also seen some validation control their we have also seen the difference between Template Model Driven and Model Driven Forms. Template Driven Forms we are few basic validators For the Model Driven Forms allows as to implements Custom Validation.

8.1 Building a Basic Login Form

login.component.ts:

Initially will be build the Login Form so it will be having Username & Password. For that purpose open the project in vs code as well as go into the project folder and executed the ng serve application currently open the URL. To create the Model Driven Forms so initially add the file in app folder login.component.ts. New file will be created inside the login.component.ts import the Component from the @angular/core file.

We used the decorator that is component, inside the component having selector & template. Selector gives the name that is 'login', and template gives the templateUrl such as 'login.component.html'. Their will be having export class LoginComponent.

```
import { Component } from "@angular/core";
@Component({
selector:'login',
templateUrl:'login.component.html'
})
export class LoginComponent{ }
```

login.component.html:

Again inside the app folder we create the login.component.html. Inside this file we create a From tag inside this div class from-group. We used the label for Username this username is input from the user input id can be username & its type will be text & this will be utilizes from controller. This will be repeated for your password, inside the label as password name will be Password again take the input id is a password, type will also be the password and Submit this value will be having the button tag class we can have "btn-btn-primary" it can have its type have Submit with label that is Login .

```
<form>
<div class="form-group">
<label for="username">Username</label>
<input id="username" type="text" class="form-control">
</div>
<div class="form-group">
<label for="password">Password</label>
<input id="password" type="password" class="form-control">
</div>
</div>
```

```
<button class="btn btn-primary" type="submit">Login</button>
</form>
```

Inside the app.component you can also include the login tag
<login> </login> and inside the your app.model.ts add the
import { LoginComponent } from './login.component';
Inside the declarations we have included the LoginComponent.

Save all. Here we can see that a login will be included with the button class. Here You can not any name here. So you can also change html form. We used the <h1> tag. We write <h1>Login Form</h1> & Save All.

Then observe the form Login Form will be shown. So if you type any inside the password filed as we type as a password that will not be show but inside the Username filed as type will be show because the type will be text.

Now we will create the different control explicitly. So to gear up our form into angular form that can perform validation. We have to create the form control & form group object. Basically form control object represented form control in form. Also we can track the value & validation state of individual form control while a form group object tracks the value & validation state of a group of form control object. So we have the form control object that can handle multiple form control. And this form control object simply represented the form control in the form, & this form group object that can control text & validation state of multiple form control. For that purpose we can modify our login component.

Login.component.ts:

Inside the login.comopent.ts first import the form group and form control from the same module that is '@angular/form'. Now use this two group so for that purpose we create the object. By calling the constructor of form group. This form group & form control are imported from the form provided form angular. Next we will asked the username and password into form group for that purpose we are passing the username & password. We also used the validators.required as soon as validators also be the import from @angular/form. The first parameter of the form control is the optional it is the default value we give to the control that means whenever you will type some username their that will be pass the particular value to the form control same as password filed.

```
import { Component } from "@angular/core";
import { FormGroup,FormControl, Validators } from "@angular/forms";
@Component({
selector:'login',
templateUrl:'login.component.html'
})
export class LoginComponent{
form = new FormGroup({
username: new FormControl(' ',Validators.required),
password: new FormControl(' ',Validators.required)
});
}
```

The first parameter in the FormControl constructor is optional. It is the default value we give to the control. This is useful when we display existing data in the control for user to edit. We first retrieve the existing value from the server and populate the control with it. The second parameter takes in a Validator function. Validators is defined in angular/commons and provides a set of validators like required, minlength and maxlength. For now, we have used Validators.required.

Back in the template, we need to tell Angular that we have created a FormGroup and its FormControls explicitly so that Angular will not create them for us as in the case of template driven forms.

login.component.html:

Next making changes in the template because of form is utilize the form group. For that purpose will be having form group. Here all the control currently it is comparing your text field for username, password and we have button. So all the control will be included in the form group. Those will be refer by using form as well as to make control available explicitly we can have this form control specify explicitly. You can give the form explicitly name that is formControlName as 'username'. Similarly you can define your password field, you can have formControlName as 'password'.

Next our template we used the validation. We can have multiple validation as a previous chapter. We have used a ngIf for validation in similar manner here we used 'ngIf' the matching condition is "form.control.username.touched && !form.control.username.valid" will be having class is a 'alert alert-danger' & you can have massage display as 'Username is required' similar for this password filed.

```
<form [formGroup]="form">
<h1>Login Form</h1>
<div class="form-group">
<label for="username">Username</label>
<input id="username" type="text" class="form-control"
formControlName="username">
</div>
<div class="form-group">
<label for="password">Password</label>
<input id="password" type="password" class="form-control"
formControlName="password">
</div>
<button class="btn btn-primary" type="submit">Login</button>
</form>
```

8.2 Implementing Validation

Next, we define validation message placeholders that will be displayed when the input is invalid.

```
<form [formGroup]="form">
<div class="form-group">
<label for="username">Username</label>
<input type="text" class="form-control" formControlName="username">
<div *ngIf="form.controls.username.touched && !form.controls.username.valid" class="alert alert-danger">
Username is required
</div>
</div>
<div class="form-group">
<label for="password">Password</label>
<input type="password" class="form-control" formControlName="password">
<div *ngIf="form.controls.password.touched && !form.controls.password.valid" class="alert alert-danger">
Password is required
</div>
</div>
<button class="btn btn-primary" type="submit">Login</button>
</form>
```

We check username css classes touched and valid to see if the control has been touched and input value is not valid. If so, display the div validation placeholder message "Username is required" with alert and alert-danger bootstrap classes. We do the same for password.

app.module.ts:

Inside the app.module.ts import the ReactiveFormsModule and also be added inside imports array.

```
import { BrowserModule } from '@angular/platform-browser';
```

```
import { NgModule } from '@angular/core';
import { ReactiveFormsModule } from '@angular/forms';
import { AppComponent } from './app.component';
import { LoginComponent } from './login.component';
@NgModule({
declarations: [
AppComponent,
],
imports: [
BrowserModule,
ReactiveFormsModule
],
providers: [],
bootstrap: [AppComponent]
})
export class AppModule { }
```

8.3 Using FormBuilder

We can use the FormBuilder class to declare FormControl and FormGroup objects in a more compact way. For example, the previous form can also be implemented with FormBuilder

login.component.html:

Now submit your values using the submit event. If you handle the submit event in the form we bind the ngSubmit. So again edit the code. Our templet here be having ngsubmit directive with the method login.

```
<form [formGroup]="form" (ngSubmit)="login()">
```

Whenever user click the submit button login() directive will be called to the login function. Now in login.component.ts, we implement the login method.

```
import { Component } from '@angular/core';
import { FormBuilder, FormGroup, FormControl, Validators } from '@angular/forms';
@Component({
selector:'login',
templateUrl: 'login.component.html'
})
export class LoginComponent {
form: FormGroup;
constructor(fb: FormBuilder){
this.form = fb.group({
username:['',Validators.required],
password:['',Validators.required]
})
}
login(){
console.log(this.form.value);
}}
```

We first import the FormBuilder class from @angular/forms. Because we are no longer using FormControl class, we can remove it from the import. In the constructor, we use dependency injection to get an instance of FormBuilder, fb. FormBuilder has a method group which takes in a shortened code for new FormControl. Essentially, FormBuilder is syntactic sugar that shortens the new FormGroup() , new FormControl() code that can build up in larger forms.

This results in cleaner and more compact for large forms. Like new FormControl, the first element is the default value and the second element is the validator function. Note that both are optional and it is not mandatory to specify them. Finally, the group method returns a FormGroup object as a result and we store it in form.

Passwordvalidator.ts:

Next, we apply the cannotContainSpace validator to the password field. Back in login.component.ts

Login.component.ts:-

Here login definition can be include in our login.component.ts file. So here we will be having login method is find of the submit event.

```
import { Component } from '@angular/core';
import { FormBuilder, FormGroup, Validators } from '@angular/forms';
import { PasswordValidator } from './passwordValidator';
@Component({
selector:'login',
templateUrl: 'login.component.html'
})
export class LoginComponent {
form: FormGroup;
constructor(fb: FormBuilder){
this.form = fb.group({
username:['',Validators.required],
password:['',Validators.compose([Validators.required,
PasswordValidator.cannotContainSpace])]
})
}
login(){
console.log(this.form.value);
}
}}
```

First, we import our PasswordValidator, and apply it to password. Because we have more than one validator on password form control, we need to compose the multiple validators by calling Validators compose method. The compose method takes in an array of Validators.

8.4 Implementing Custom Validation

Try to implement custom validation into password field. Just for example most of the cases creating a password the password length will be minimum of 6 character or 8 character. So how it can be done so we create the file called the passwordvalidator.ts. This is your custom validation. Inside that this file import the formcontrol from angular form. Now export class passwordvalidator inside class defining the cannotcontainspace() method will be used to check the inside password can contain any Space. So we created the form control reference here.

```
import { FormControl } from "@angular/forms";
export class PasswordValidator{
static cannotContainSpace(formControl: FormControl){
if(formControl.value.indexOf('')>=0)
return{cannotContainSpace:true};
return null;
}
}
```

We declare a static method cannotContainSpace that takes in a FormControl object as argument. We access the value string property of the formControl and check if there are spaces in it with the indexOf method. If there are, we return { cannotContainSpace: true } and if there are not spaces, we return null.

login.component.html:

Finally, we implement the custom validation message placeholder. Back in login.component.html, replace the validation codes for password

```
<form [formGroup]="form" (ngSubmit)="login()">
<div class="form-group">
<label for="username">Username</label>
<input type="text" class="form-control" formControlName="username">
<div *ngIf="form.controls.username.touched
&& !form.controls.username.valid" class="alert alert-danger">
Username is required
</div>
</div>
<div class="form-group">
<label for="password">Password</label>
<input type="password" class="form-control" formControlName="password">
<div *ngIf="form.controls.password.touched
&& form.controls.password.errors">
<div *ngIf="form.controls.password.errors.required"
class="alert alert-danger">
Password is required.
</div>
<div *ngIf="form.controls.password.errors.cannotContainSpace"
class="alert alert-danger">
Password cannot contain space.
</div>
</div>
</div>
<button class="btn btn-primary" type="submit">Login</button>
</form>
```

8.5 Validating Upon Form Submit

First in app folder, create a new file login.service.ts which is the service class for login functionality. Remember that we should implement logic in service classes to keep our component classes lightweight and mainly for rendering displays. Fill in login.service.ts

```
import {Injectable} from '@angular/core';
@Injectable()
export class LoginService {
login(username, password){
if(username === "jason" && password === "123")
return true;
else
return false;
}
}
```

login.component.ts:

```
import { Component } from '@angular/core';
import { FormBuilder, FormGroup, Validators } from '@angular/forms';
import { PasswordValidator } from './passwordValidator';
import { LoginService } from './login.service';
@Component({
selector:'login',
templateUrl: 'login.component.html'
})
export class LoginComponent {
form: FormGroup;
constructor(fb: FormBuilder, private _loginService: LoginService){
this.form = fb.group({
username:['',Validators.required ],
password:['',Validators.compose([Validators.required,
PasswordValidator.cannotContainSpace])]
})
}
login(){
var result = this._loginService.login(this.form.controls['username'].value,
this.form.controls['password'].value);
if(!result){
this.form.controls['password'].setErrors({
invalidLogin: true
});
}
}
}
```

In this chapter, we learnt how to implement model driven forms in Angular. We learnt how to create FormControl and FormGroup objects, use FormBuilder to make our code more compact, how to implement custom validation, and how to validate the form upon submit. Now after submitting a form, we need to persist the data by calling the api endpoint of the server.

User Form
First Name
Email
country
Login Form
Username
Kiran
Password
Password cannot Contain Space
Login

CHAPTER NINE

Introduction to Observables

In previous chapter we discussed about the model driven form and template driven form. In this chapter we well discus about Observables.

For Angular to connect to backend servers we required Observables, which is a concept introduced in a library called Reactive extensions. Reactive Extensions is a comprehensive library by itself independent from Angular. If you wish to know more about it, you can go to reactivex.io. Reactive Extensions have been implemented for Java, Javascript, .Net, Scala, Clojure, Swift and other languages. Reactive Extensions is used in a few parts of Angular especially in the classes we use to connect to a server. The rxjs folder in node_modules contains the Reactive Extensions library for Javascript used by Angular.

9.1 Observables

Observables are at the core of Reactive Extensions. An Observable represents an asynchronous data stream where data arrives asynchronously. An example is the keyup event from a textbox. Another example is a web socket. A server uses web-sockets to send data to the client. Data arrives asynchronously and we can model it as an Observable stream.

There is separate folder which is referred as rxjs. This rxjs folder available inside node_modules contain reactive extension javascript library used by angular.

We can think of Observables as a collection. The difference is that in a collection we iterate through the collection and pull each object one at a time

```
foreach(var obj in collection){
...
}
```

For an Observable stream, we subscribe to it and give it a callback function.

```
function(newData){
...
}
```

When a new data element arrives, it will push that data element to us by calling the provided function back. We thus call the provided function a callback function. We observe Observable streams and get notified when data arrives asynchronously, we call them Observables.

How to create Observable ,

9.2 Creating an Observable from DOM Events

We will illustrate Observables by creating an Observable stream from the keyup event of a textbox. Suppose we want to implement a search service to look up artists' data on spotify.com. We do this by typing a search term into the input box and then call the spotify api to get artists data with a similar name.

First, either re-use the project you have from previous chapters or create a new project using to implement to Observable. Inside the project folder Again you can go to app.component.ts you can have the form control here including one search text box

```
import { Component } from '@angular/core';
import { FormControl } from '@angular/forms';
@Component({
selector: 'app-root',
template: `
<input class="form-control" type="search"
[formControl]="searchControl">
`
})
export class AppComponent {
searchControl = new FormControl();
constructor(){
this.searchControl.valueChanges.subscribe(value => {
console.log(value);
});
}
}
```

Because our search input consists of just one input control, we do not need a Top of Form element for it. We can use the formControl directive in the input control. The formControl represents our input field.

```
<input class="form-control" type="search"
[formControl]="searchControl">
```

The formControl class has a property valueChanges (see below) which returns an Observable. We can subscribe to this observable by calling the subscribe method. In this way, we get notified whenever the value in the input field changes.

```
constructor() {
this.searchControl.valueChanges.subscribe(value => {
console.log(value);
});
}
```

The subscribe method requires a function as argument. This function will be called by the Observable when new data arrives (i.e. value in input field changes). You can declare a function using the traditional anonymous function syntax like

```
function (value){
console.log(value);
}
```

or you can shorten this code and use the arrow function (or lambda expression syntax).

```
value => {
console.log(value);
}
```

Every time we press a key in the textbox, we get the text value pushed to us in an Observable stream. Our callback function gets called and we print the value to the console

For that purpose we start debugging here, so we can have debug console open your application in browser. for every value inside the search filed that we get observe using Observable. In search box we write the Hello Kiran String. We observed this string in console.

Pass String

Login Form

Username

Password

Login

Hello Kiran

Console Observed

```
})
export class AppComponent {
  title:String = 'My_Proj: Seventh Session -Template Driven Forms.';
  imageUrl="https://picsum.photos/800/400";
  isActive=true;
  searchControl = new FormControl();
  constructor(){
    this.searchControl.valueChanges.pipe(
    filter(text=>text.length>=4),
    debounceTime(400),
    distinctUntilChanged())
    .subscribe(value=>{
      console.log(value);
    });
  }
  onClick($event:any){
    console.log("Clicked",$event)
```

9.3 Observable Operators

So what are the benefit of Observables? The benefit of Observables are that it provides a set of operators that we can use to transform, filter, aggregate and combine data received from the observable stream. In the following, we look at some of the operators: filter Operator In our input, say we want to call Spotify only if the user types at least three characters so as not to flood Spotify with too many requests. To do so, we can apply the filter operator. We do so by first importing the filter operator with the below code

```
import 'rxjs/add/operator/filter'; and add the filter operator
this.searchControl.valueChanges
.filter(text => text.length >= 3)
.subscribe(value => {
console.log(value);
});
```

The filter operator takes an expression text.length >= 3 and determines that the value should be selected only if the expression returns true. filter then returns another Observable that we can either subscribe to or apply another operator. If we run the app now, we see only text of length greater or equal to three logged in the console.

debounceTime Operator

Suppose we want to wait 400 milliseconds in between requests before calling Spotify, we can apply the debounceTime operator. We do so by first importing the debounceTime operator with the below code

```
import 'rxjs/add/operator/debounceTime';
```

Next, we add the debounceTime operator

```
this.searchControl.valueChanges
.filter(text => text.length >= 3)
.debounceTime(400)
.subscribe(value => {
console.log(value);
});
```

distinctUntilChanged Operator

Say if a user presses theleft and right arrow keys to move the cursor, the valueChange event is fired and we send multiple requests with the same input string to Spotify since the text in the input field is not changed. To avoid such multiple requests with the same search term, we can apply the distinctUntilChanged operator which will let us receive our Observable only when the text is changed. We do so by first importing the distinctUntilChanged operator with the below code

```
import 'rxjs/add/operator/distinctUntilChanged';
```

Next, add the distinctUntilChanged operator

```
this.searchControl.valueChanges
.filter(text => text.length >= 3)
.debounceTime(400)
.distinctUntilChanged()
.subscribe(value => {
console.log(value);
});
```

Final Code

Below shows the final code for our app component.

```
import { Component } from '@angular/core';
import { Observable } from 'rxjs/Rx';
import 'rxjs/add/operator/filter';
import 'rxjs/add/operator/debounceTime';
import 'rxjs/add/operator/distinctUntilChanged';
import { FormControl } from '@angular/forms';
```

```
@Component({
selector: 'app-root',
template: `
<input class="form-control" type="search"
[formControl]="searchControl">
`
})
export class AppComponent {
searchControl = new FormControl();
constructor(){
this.searchControl.valueChanges
.filter(text => text.length >= 3)
.debounceTime(400)
.distinctUntilChanged()
.subscribe(value => {
console.log(value);
});
}
}
```

In this chapter, we are introduced to Observables, how to subscribe to Observables from DOM events, and how to apply certain Observable operator.

CHAPTER TEN

Communicating with Server with Spotify API

Welcome to Chapter 10 on angular and typescript. In this Chapter we'll be discussing how to connect to server. So basically in previous Chapter we have seen how to subscribe to observable. So we'll see how to call backend services to get data through restful API.

It will be covering: RESTful API, Getting Data from the Server, Dependency Injection, Component's Lifecycle Hooks, OnInit, OnDestroy, DoCheck, OnChanges, AfterContentInit, AfterContentChecked, AfterViewInit, AfterViewChecked, Showing a Loader Icon, Spotify Results Display Page, Adding an Input to Spotify Results Display Page, RESTful API using Observables, Http, HttpClient, HttpClientModule, get(), post(), put(), delete(), head()

10.1 A Simple RESTful API

This application programming interface will be using to get the data from backend services so this restful API is also known as representational state transfer. So this representational state transfer is a is architectural style that describes uniform interface between the physically separated components. So these components or you can say physical system often across the internet basically in client and server architecture. So this restful API provides an interface through which two computer system used to exchange information securely over the Internet. This restful API are used in most of the business application to communicate with other internal and third party application to perform various tasks . So simple restful API building a restful API basically the complete restful API is beyond the scope of angular because when you are talking about angular so it is let's client side technology. Whereas if you want to build restful API. So they building like restfully required server side technology. Such as you can take example of node.js it is server side technology. Even asp.net also the example of rupee on the rails, python, Django, flask, PHP all this can be used for developing restful API.

So Will illustrate in this Chapter by connecting to Spotify restful API to retrieve and manage the contents of Spotify. So you can know more about this Spotify API on this URL that https://developer.spotify.com/documentation/web-api/ documentation Web API are these Spotify app provides. You can say various artist you can see contents are produced by artists or if you can search those contents so these are General songs. So this we'll be trying to fetch the contents of Spotify using these Spotify Web API. So here you can see that we'll be developing an application so there is your application here it is spotify.com and using Spotify web application interface will be fetching data from Spotify so this this Web API.

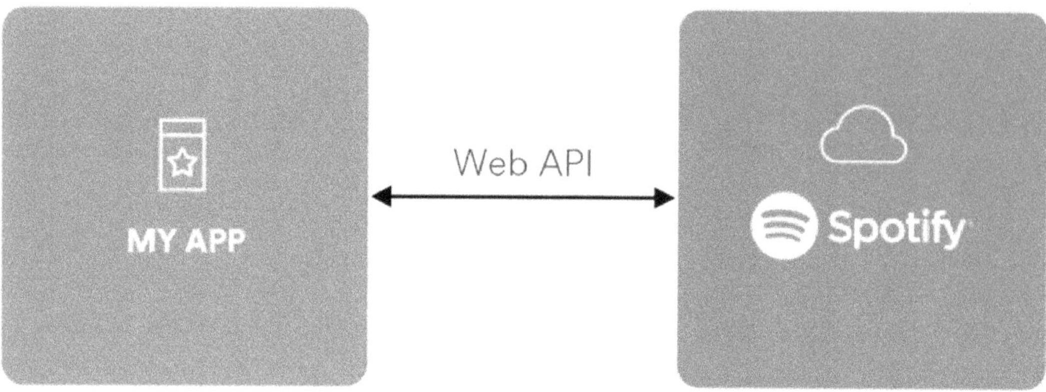

This Web API provided by Spotify is based on simple rest principle. So it is a representational state transfer. So why it is representational State transfer so that data can be used to represent the data fetched from the server so the Spotify Web API endpoints written in Json metadata about you can say music artist album tracks and it can be fetch from directly from the Spotify data catalog. So when you are talking about Json. Json is a stands for the JavaScript object notations. Json so this Spotify API will be returning data in Json format so this is nothing but the JavaScript object notation.

Json is lightweight data interchange format basically it is plain text written in JavaScript object notation so it is preferably used for storing temporary data. Whatever data that we are fetching for Spotify that will be stored inside Json format and that will be utilizing to show the contents of our application the application that will be developing here. You can also access the API here just for example if you want to because we will be searching the name of artist in the search box and our application will be displaying the list of artists with the name of artist for which was searched so here if you go to console so inside this console you have searched where you have this get method for API here you can see the endpoint API here. You will be using this URL that is https://api.spotify.com/v1/search and we'll try to get the response in Json format and we'll try to create the artists name. Whenever I am typing the or modifying the parameters here for that API so you can see that these gate URL getting changed. When I typed here under ‘ q ’ the Json so here in front of search URL you have question mark ‘ q ’ is the Json and if I type here artist. So you will see here changes that is type is equals to artists so our search query will be comprising or will be returning the Json format of the search artist.

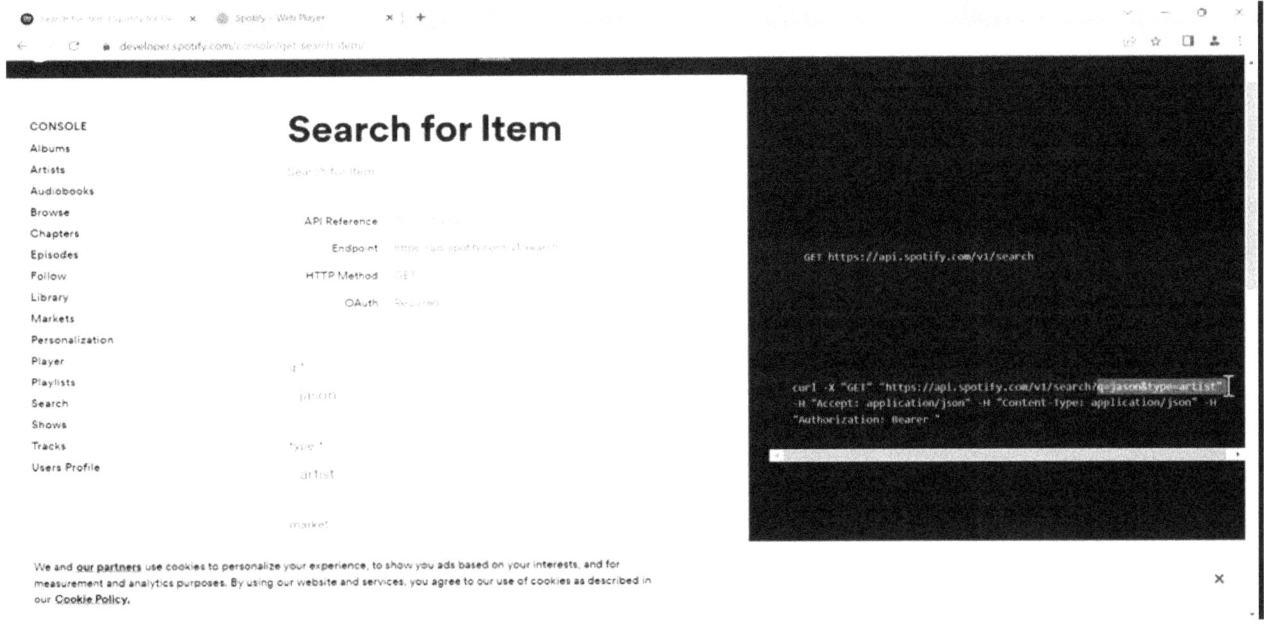

10.2 Getting Data from the Server

Now how to get the data from this server. Let's discuss I'm getting data from data server so to get data using restful API. We are going to use the HTTP class. This class is provided in angular which used to make the Ajax calls to server using this HTTP class. So basically this HTTP class provides various methods that you can use along with the object of that HTTP class and it will be the used to make the Ajax calls to the server. What is Ajax again asynchronous JavaScript and XML .

Whenever you want data in this JavaScript & XML format call can be made to the server using HTTP class. So this HTTP class provides various methods such as ,

- get()- method for getting a resource from the server
- post()- method for creating
- put()- method for updating the resource
- delete()- method for deleting resource
- head()- method for getting metadata regarding the resource

All these methods can be used which are provided by the HTTP class. We are basically interested in getting data from this server. We'll be using this get() method. Somewhere you want to post the query search query. In that case you can use post() method. First we'll create a service which will responsible for talking to our restful API. Our component should not make HTTP calls directly rather delegate that role to services.

Spotify.service.ts

For that purpose again we'll go to our project again here you can create separate project you can open the existing project that we had created. Inside the app folder you can have service created for this Spotify we'll create this service by giving it name as **Spotify.service.ts.** So we have created this file Spotify. In app folder and Initially import. We will be using http class. Here you will be using HTTP class that you can import from the angular HTTP library. Similarly you have import Map from the rxjs from the Operators.

Next in this particular Spotify service we will be using defining a class name as SpotifyService. Take the Constructor of it here we'll be taking a private members http. Generally whenever you are declaring any private members. It is General practice to start it with underscore but it is not compulsory. So it is of http. Inside that we will have this Constructor declared here and a method for getting data from the Spotify. So this is again the user defined method we are defining it with name get Spotify data and return **this._http.get** pass here the URL that is https://api.spotify.com/v1/search?q=jackson&type=artist. Once our search it will return in Json format search comprising all artists so that can be passed here. Next will be the **.map** and again we will be having resources switch from the Json that has been written so this is how you can use it here.

```
import {Http} from '@angular/http';
import 'rxjs/add/operator/map';
export class SpotifyService{
constructor(private _http: Http){
}
getSpotifyData(){
return this._http.get("https://api.spotify.com/v1/search?q=jason&type=artist")
.map(res => res.json())
}
}
```

Now this gets Spotify data is a method that will return Spotify data from our API endpoint. You can also see that the end point API input end we are searching some different items here.

This query parameter that we have passed to it then to call our API endpoint. We need to use HTTP service of angular. We input it using this angular slash HTTP so this HTTP has been imported from and we inject the HTTP class into the Constructor here of our Spotify service. Then there should be dependency injection let angular create an instance of HTTP class and give it to us. Our Constructor has parent parameter. This private parameter is there underscore HTTP which is of type HTTP.

By convention we prefix any private field with the underscore. In get Spotify data we use the get method here of HTTP and give the URL of our API endpoint. So we are currently hard coding our search term to be Json. This will be changed letter when we use the search term provided by the user from input. Here we have hard coded the search query as Json so the artist name will be Json that will be utilized. Then even it will be returning the response in the Json format.

Here again you can use it as any types as a data type. So our component will be a consumer of this observable. Here you can see that when we use the search term provided by the user for the input it will be returning the response. So the return type of this get method is an observable of a response. Currently we are taking it as the HTTP response from the server. So we'll return this observable in our service and our component will be the consumer of this observable. We will subscribe to it and when another call is completed the response is spread to the observable and then pushed to the component. For again further we use this map operatable to transform our response object into the Json type. So whatever response written by the get method that is nothing but the HTTP response will be returned and that will be converted or transform into Json type by this map method. Now we will try to insert the dependency.

10.3 Dependency Injection

Next, we inject our service into our component. As covered in chapter 7, we do so by first marking our Spotify service class as available for dependency injection. We decorate it with the @Injectable() annotation

```
import {Http} from '@angular/http';
import 'rxjs/add/operator/map';
import { Injectable } from '@angular/core';
@Injectable()
```

```
export class SpotifyService{
constructor(private _http: Http){
}
getSpotifyData(){
return this._http
.get("https://api.spotify.com/v1/search?q=jason&type=artist")
.map(res => res.json());
}
}
```

Remember that in dependency injection, Angular looks at the constructor and sees a parameter of type SpotifyService and seeks to create an instance of it. To let the injector know where to find the SpotifyService to create it, we register the SpotifyService by specifying it in the providers property in the component's metadata. Now that we are done with the dependency injection, let's use our service. In the constructor, we call the getSpotifyData method from our _sportifyService instance. The getSpotifyData method returns an Observable which we need to subscribe to. We then pass in our callback function data =>console.log(data). Back in the implementation of getSpotifyData, we use the map method to transform the response into a json object. So when our ajax call is completed, a json object is placed in the observable and then pushed into our callback function.

10.4 Component's Lifecycle Hooks

Even though our code currently works, it doesn't follow best practises. We are currently calling the server in the constructor of the app component. As a best practise, constructors should be lightweight and should not contain any costly operations making it easier to test and debug. So where should we move our code to? Components have a lifecycle which is managed by Angular. There are lifecycle hooks which we can tap into during key moments in the component's lifecycle. To do this, we need to implement one or more of the following interfaces in the component. Such as,

- OnInit
- OnDestroy
- DoCheck
- OnChanges
- AfterContentInit
- AfterContentChecked
- AfterViewInit
- AfterViewChecked

Each of the interfaces has a method that we can implement in our component. When the right moment arrives, Angular will call these methods. For example, we can implement the OnInit interface to be notified when a component is first instantiated. By convention, the name of the method is the same name as the interface with the prefix ng. For e.g. ngOnInit. We will implement the ngOnInit() method. This method will be called when Angular instantiates our component. In terms of lifecycle, it is called after the constructor. So in the constructor, we do lightweight and basic initialization and if we need to call the server, we do it in ngOnInit. So we shift the code to call Spotify from the constructor to ngOnInit.

```
export class AppComponent {
constructor(private _spotifyService: SpotifyService){
}
ngOnInit() {
this._spotifyService.getSpotifyData()
```

```
.subscribe(data => console.log(data.artists.items));
}
}
```

10.5 Showing a Loader Icon

When getting content from a server, it is often useful to show a loading icon to the user. To do so, in app component, create a variable called isLoading and set it to true like in the below code.

```
export class AppComponent {
isLoading = true;
...
```

Next, in the subscribe method, set isLoading to false because at this point, we get the results from the server and loading is finished.

```
ngOnInit() {
this._spotifyService.getSpotifyData()
.subscribe(data => {
this.isLoading = false;
console.log(this.artists);
});
}
```

If you load your app in the browser, you should see the “Getting data” message being displayed for a short moment before data from the server is loaded. We will now replace the “Getting data” message with the loading icon. To get the loading icon, google ‘font awesome’ and the first result should be http://fontawesome.io/.

Font awesome is a library similar to glyphicons that gives us many useful icons. Go to ‘Get Started’ and follow the instructions to copy the embed code and paste it into the head section of index.html . Back in app component, replace the message with the icon like in the below code.

```
template: `
<div *ngIf="isLoading">
<i class="fa fa-spinner fa-spin fa-3x"></i>
</div> `,
```

To add a font awesomeicon, we use the *tag. fa is the base class for all font awesome icons.* fa-spinner renders the spinner icon. fa-spin adds the animation to it. fa-3x makes the icon three times bigger so that it is easier to see.

10.6 Implementing a Spotify Results Display Page

We will now implement a page which displays our Spotify data nicely like in following screenshot. To do so, we use the Bootstrap Media Object component from http://getbootstrap.com/components/#media as what we have done previously. We will be copying the markup from getbootstrap, pasting it into our component and filling the missing parts with interpolation strings.

Firstly, note that the images that we get from Spotify are of different height and width. To make all images of different height and width display the same in our page for e.g. 100px by 100px, we define the following inline css style class img.

```
@Component({
selector: 'app-root',
styles: [`
.img {
position: relative;
float: left;
width: 100px;
height: 100px;
background-position: 50% 50%;
background-repeat: no-repeat;
background-size: cover;
}
`],
```

In the template, we will be copy the markup from getbootstrap and paste it into our component

```
template: `
template: `
<h3>Spotify Results</h3>
<div *ngIf="isLoading">
<i class="fa fa-spinner fa-spin fa-3x"></i>
</div>
<div *ngFor="let artist of artists" class="media">
<div class="media-left">
<a href="#">
<img class="media-object img"
src="{{ artist.images[2]?.url }}" alt="...">
```

```
</a>
</div>
<div class="media-body">
<h4 class="media-heading">{{ artist.name }}</h4>
Followers: {{ artist.followers.total}}
Popularity: {{ artist.popularity }}
</div>
</div>
`,
```

We then apply *ngFor to repeat the media object for each artist we get from Spotify. We then add four string interpolations inside the template. The artist's name, image, number of followers and her popularity. Note that Spotify displays larger image sizes in the first few elements of the image array. I therefore use the third element i.e. artist.images[2]?.url for a reasonably appropriate image size. You can of course change this to use the first or second element if you want. Not all artist however have images. And you might get an error if you try to display an artist that does have an image array. To handle this, we add the ? operator after the field to specify that it is optional.

In our *ngFor, we state let artist of artists. But where do we get our artists array instantiated and assigned with content? We declare it in app component artists = [] as shown below. We then subscribe to our Observable returned from our Spotify service and assign the returned result to artists array. Note that we assign it with data.artists.items as this is the artists item array structured in the json response.

```
export class AppComponent {
isLoading = true;
artists = [];
constructor(private _spotifyService: SpotifyService){
}
ngOnInit() {
this._spotifyService.getSpotifyData()
.subscribe(data => {
this.isLoading = false;
this.artists = data.artists.items;
console.log(this.artists);
});
}
}
```

10.7 Adding an Input to Spotify Results Display Page

We are currently hard-coding our search term to jason in the url used to request from Spotify. We will now use the search input that we have implemented in chapter 8 and combine it with our code here so that as a user types in her search terms, the result can be displayed.

The final app component code will look like below. Note that we initialize isLoading to false at first since no call to Spotify is made at the beginning. Once we get a notification from valueChanges Observable, we then set isLoading to true just before the call to getSpotifyData to show the loading icon. Once we get notified of results from our spotify service Observable, we set isLoading to false to hide the loading icon.

```
export class AppComponent {
searchControl = new FormControl();
isLoading = false;
artists = [];
constructor(private _spotifyService: SpotifyService){
}
ngOnInit() {
this.searchControl.valueChanges
.filter(text => text.length >= 3)
.debounceTime(400)
.distinctUntilChanged()
.subscribe(value => {
this.isLoading = true;
this._spotifyService.getSpotifyData(value)
.subscribe(data => {
this.isLoading = false;
this.artists = data.artists.items;
});
});
}
}
```

In the chapter, we learned how to implement a Spotify Search application by connecting our Angular apps to the server RESTful api using Observables, Http, component lifecycle hooks and display loader icons.

CHAPTER ELEVEN

C.R.U.D with FireBase

We will discuss how to build complete C.R.U.D. procedures in Angular using a backend server in this chapter. The server side and client side make up the usual web application architecture. This book shows you how to use Angular to implement the client side. Through RESTful http services created with server-side frameworks like ASP.NET, Node.js, and Ruby on Rails, the client side communicates with a backend server to obtain or save data. When we obtained information from the Spotify server, we looked into this.

However, developing the server side takes a lot of work and is outside the purview of this book. However, in this chapter, we'll look at using Firebase as our backend server. For creating quick and scalable real-time apps, Firebase is a highly potent backend platform. Do not worry if you have never used Firebase before; it has been growing popularity since 2015, and we will present it here.

We can create relational databases without writing server-side code thanks to Firebase. A real-time, quick, and scalable NoSQL cloud database, as well as a framework to communicate with it, are both made available to us by Firebase. As a result, we may concentrate on creating our application in accordance with the specifications rather than on fixing server-side code.

You may know that What is a NoSQL database, you might wonder? A NoSQL database has a tree of JSON objects, each of which can have a varied structure, as opposed to relational databases, which consist of tables and relationships. NoSQL databases provide us one less thing to worry about by eliminating the need to maintain table schemas, enhancing productivity. A relational database may still be a preferable option, though, if your application requires a lot of data aggregation, intricate querying, and reporting.

To enable you to develop a fully functional app, the goal of this chapter is to show create, read, update, and delete functions using Angular and Firebase combined.

12.1 More About FireBase

- Firebase is a platform developed by Google that provides a variety of services for developing and managing mobile and web applications.
- Firebase services include:
    - Realtime Database: A cloud-based database that allows for real-time data synchronization between client and server.
    - Cloud Fire store: A newer database service that offers more features and flexibility than the Realtime Database.
    - Cloud Storage: A cloud-based storage service for storing user data, such as images, videos, and files.
    - Cloud Functions: A serverless platform that allows developers to run code in response to events, such as user activity or changes to data.
    - Authentication: A service that provides user authentication and authorization.
    - Cloud Messaging: A service that allows developers to send push notifications to users.
    - Analytics: A service that provides insights into user behaviour and app usage.

- Firebase is a popular choice for developing mobile and web applications because it provides a comprehensive set of features that can be used to build complex applications. Firebase is also easy to use and can be integrated with a variety of development platforms.

12.2 Here are some of the benefits of using Firebase

- **Realtime data synchronization:** Firebase provides real-time data synchronization between client and server, which means that users will always see the latest data. This is ideal for applications that require users to collaborate in real time, such as social media apps or games.
- **Scalability:** Firebase is designed to scale to meet the needs of even the most demanding applications. As your app grows in popularity, Firebase will automatically scale your database and storage to meet the demand.
- **Security:** Firebase is built on Google's infrastructure, which means that your data is secure and reliable. Firebase also provides a variety of security features, such as user authentication and data encryption, to help protect your data.
- **Ease of use:** Firebase is designed to be easy to use, even for developers who are new to cloud computing. Firebase provides a variety of tools and documentation to help you get started quickly.

12.3 Using Firebase

Firebase capabilities may be used without cost, with payment only required when our application expands. Either a subscription-based plan or a "pay as you use" option is available. Visit https://firebase.google.com/ for additional information.

We must first register a Firebase account before including Firebase in our Angular app. Enter your Google account information to sign in at https://firebase.google.com/. In order to access the Firebase interface, below are the steps to activate firebase.

Step 1: Click on Get Started

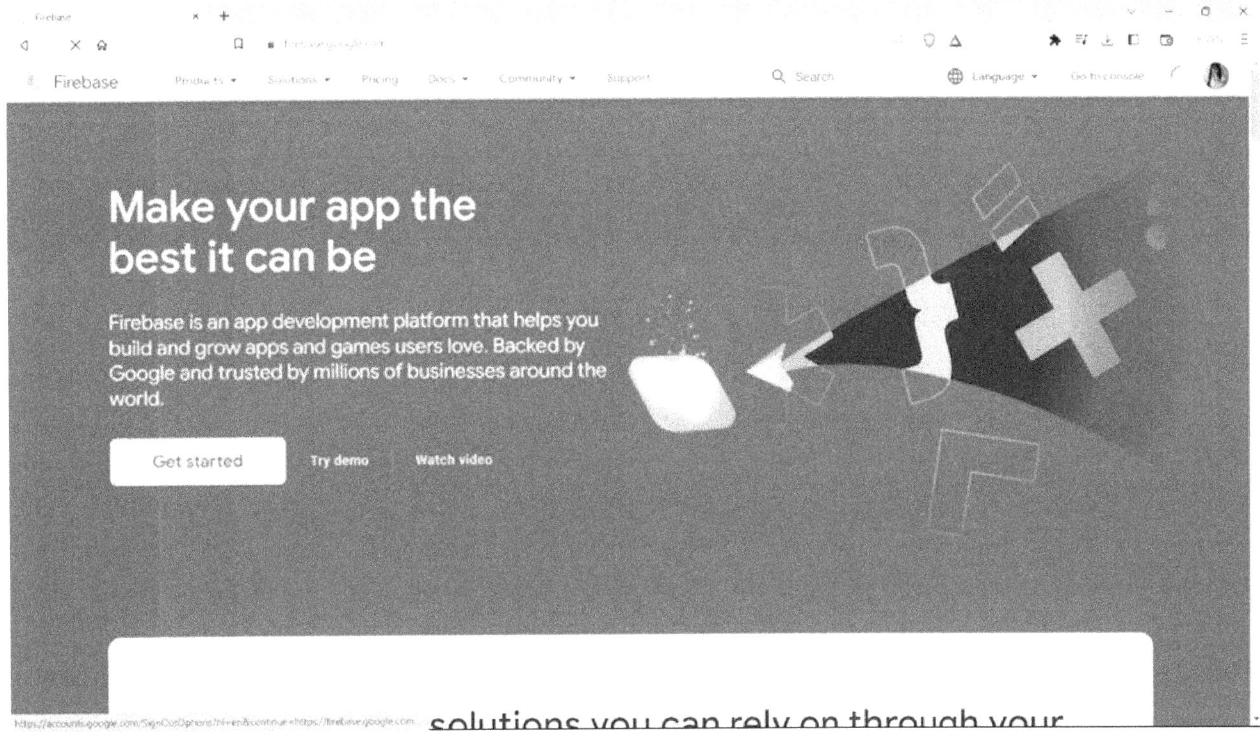

Step 2: On the welcome page click on create a project

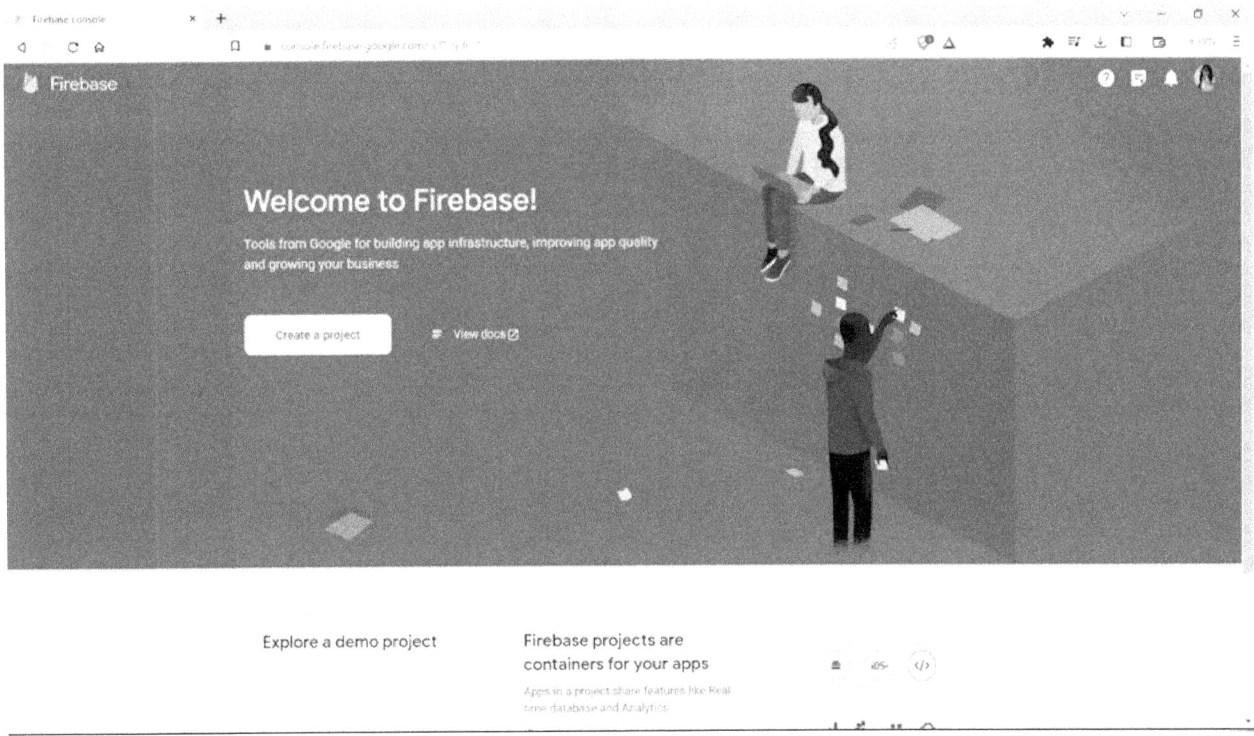

Step 3: Giving a project name to our project as CRUD-Chapter12 & accept the firebase terms then click on continue.

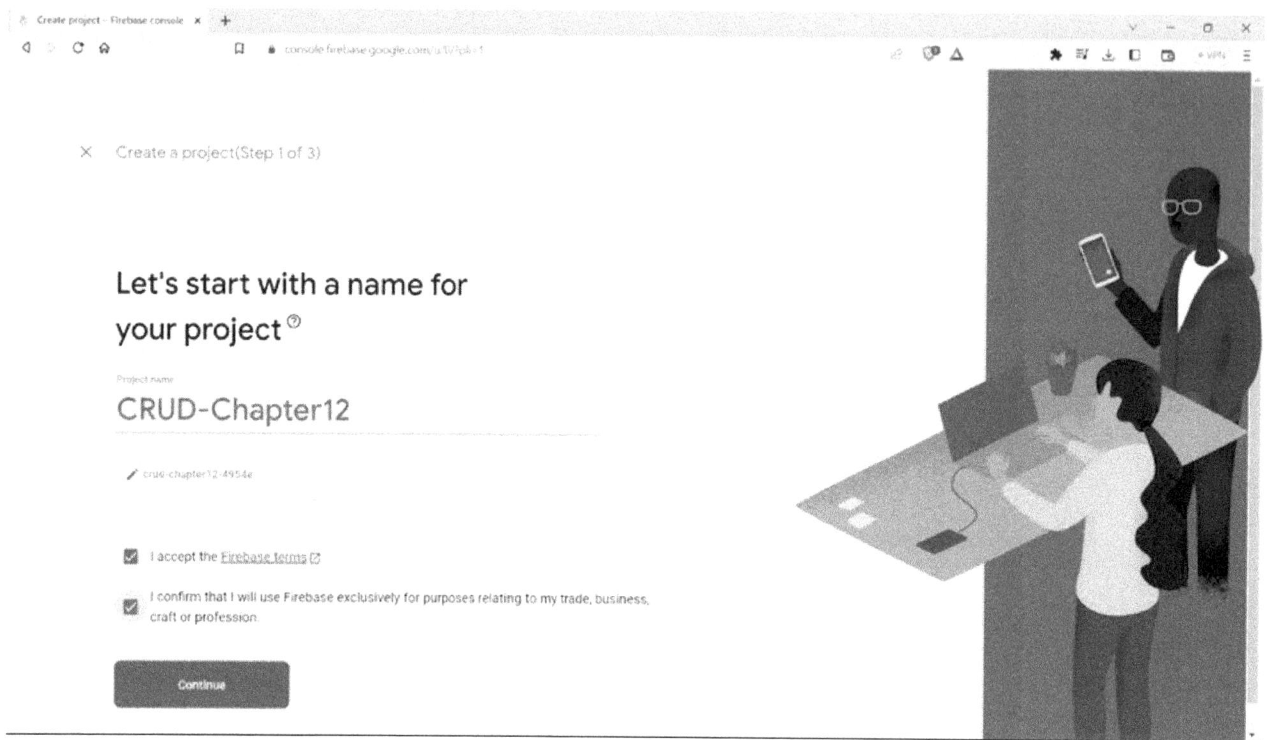

Step 4: Enabling Google Analytics for the project for targeting, reporting and more in firebase

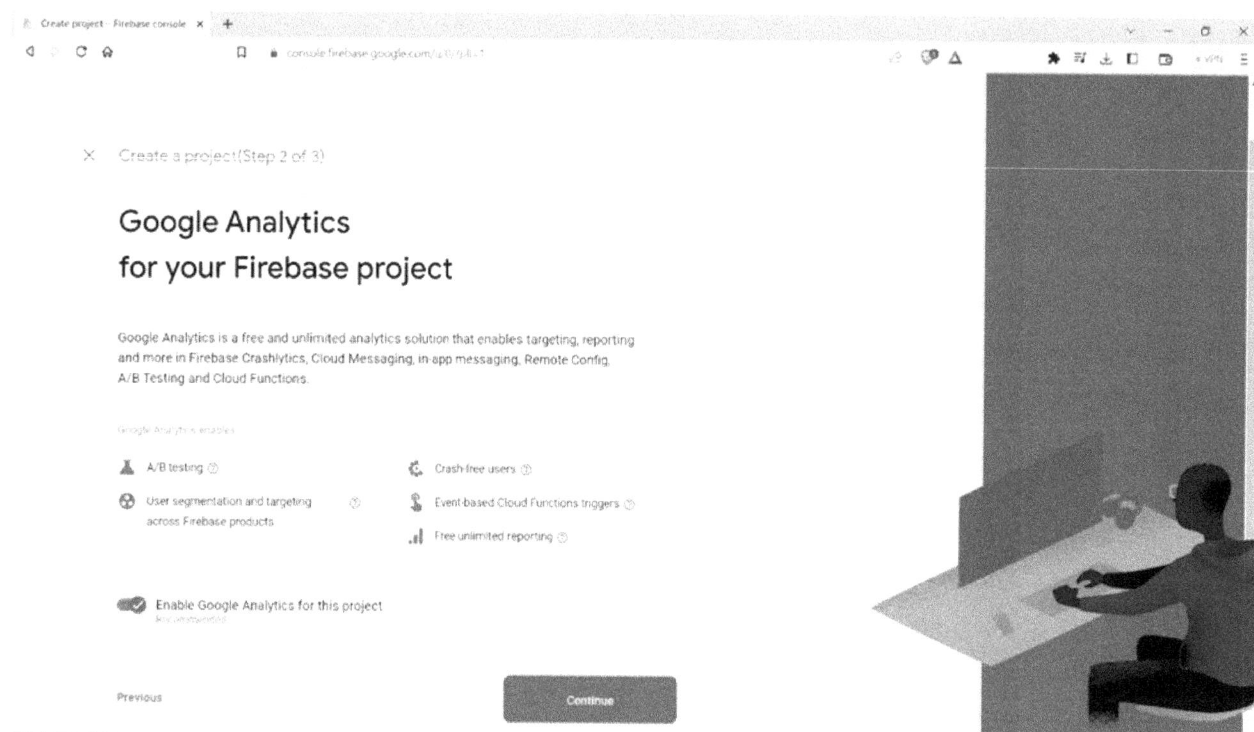

Step 5: Configuring Google Analytics and selecting location as our country then click on check mark to use the default settings and accept the google analytics terms and click on Create Project.

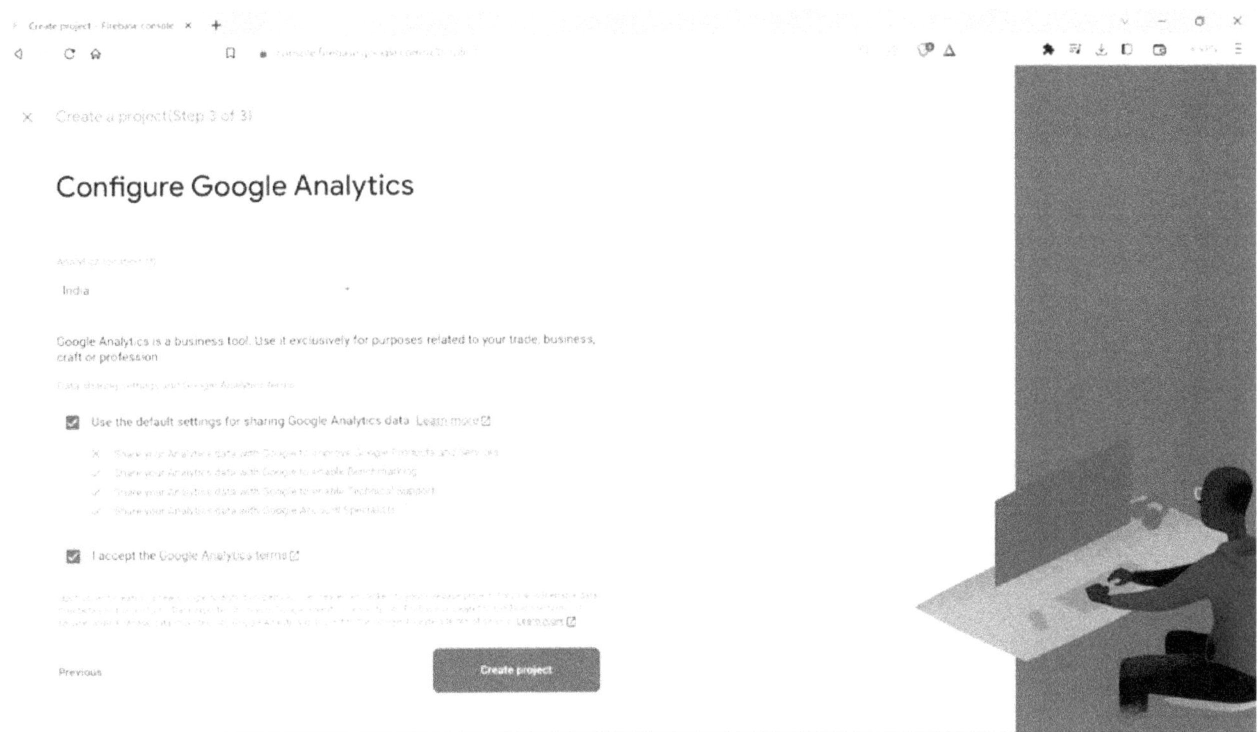

Step 6: We get an interface as your new project is ready and click on continue.

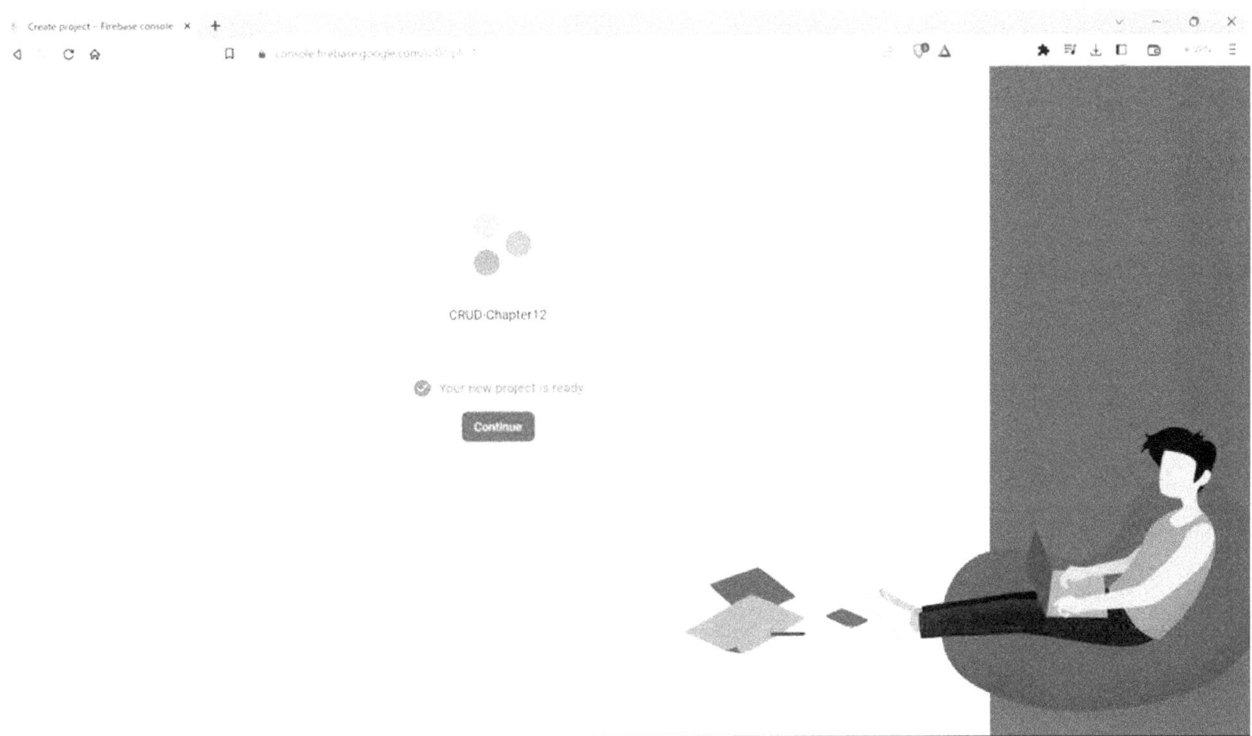

Step 7: Click on Get Started

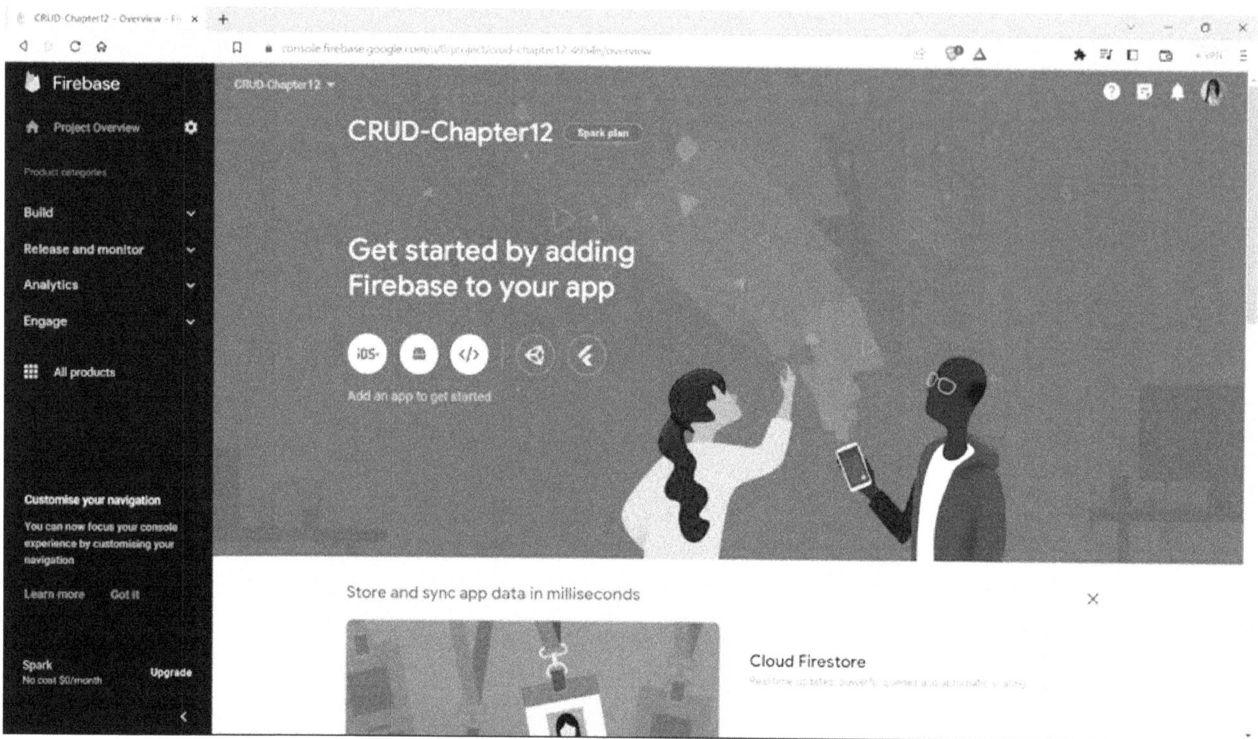

Step 8: Registering our web app with firebase ang providing nickname as CRUD-Chapter12

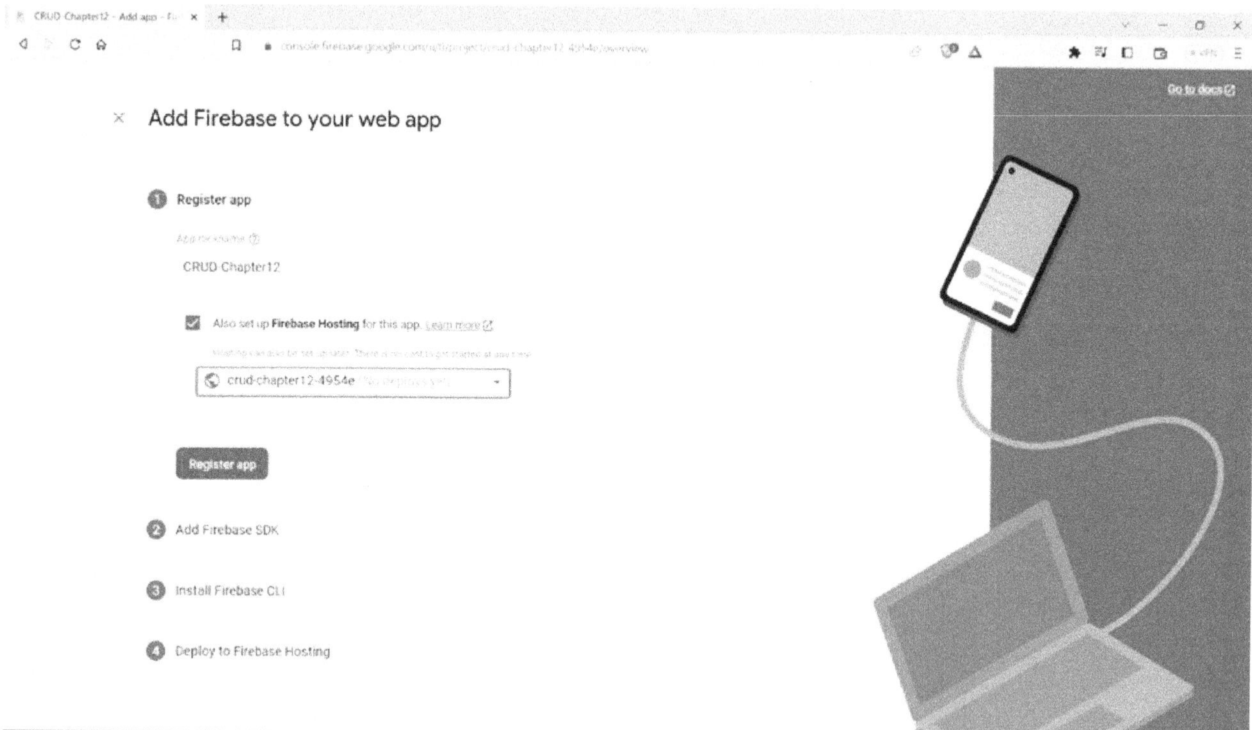

Step 9: Generated SDK Firebase code help for connecting client and server and will import in routing

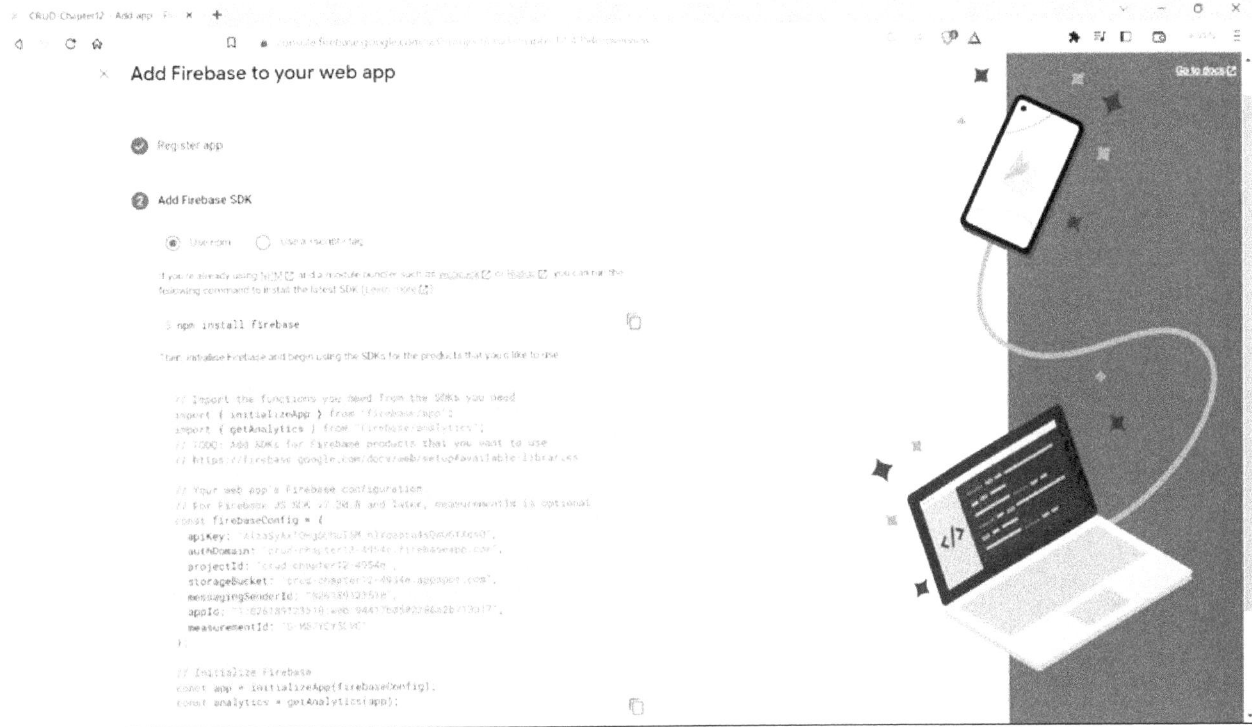

12.4 Adding Firebase to Our App

Now for connecting firebase to our angular app we will create a fresh new project using angular CLI as show below

```
C:\Users\Hp\Desktop\Angular>ng new CRUD-Chapter12
Node.js version v19.9.0 detected.
Odd numbered Node.js versions will not enter LTS status and should not be used for production. For more information, please see https://nodejs.org/en/about/
releases/.
? Would you like to add Angular routing? Yes
? Which stylesheet format would you like to use? SCSS   [ https://sass-lang.com/documentation/syntax#scss
 ]
CREATE CRUD-Chapter12/angular.json (2914 bytes)
CREATE CRUD-Chapter12/package.json (1045 bytes)
CREATE CRUD-Chapter12/README.md (1067 bytes)
CREATE CRUD-Chapter12/tsconfig.json (901 bytes)
CREATE CRUD-Chapter12/.editorconfig (274 bytes)
CREATE CRUD-Chapter12/.gitignore (548 bytes)
CREATE CRUD-Chapter12/tsconfig.app.json (263 bytes)
CREATE CRUD-Chapter12/tsconfig.spec.json (273 bytes)
CREATE CRUD-Chapter12/.vscode/extensions.json (130 bytes)
CREATE CRUD-Chapter12/.vscode/launch.json (470 bytes)
CREATE CRUD-Chapter12/.vscode/tasks.json (938 bytes)
CREATE CRUD-Chapter12/src/main.ts (214 bytes)
CREATE CRUD-Chapter12/src/favicon.ico (948 bytes)
CREATE CRUD-Chapter12/src/index.html (299 bytes)
CREATE CRUD-Chapter12/src/styles.scss (80 bytes)
CREATE CRUD-Chapter12/src/app/app-routing.module.ts (245 bytes)
CREATE CRUD-Chapter12/src/app/app.module.ts (393 bytes)
CREATE CRUD-Chapter12/src/app/app.component.html (23115 bytes)
CREATE CRUD-Chapter12/src/app/app.component.spec.ts (1015 bytes)
CREATE CRUD-Chapter12/src/app/app.component.ts (219 bytes)
CREATE CRUD-Chapter12/src/app/app.component.scss (0 bytes)
CREATE CRUD-Chapter12/src/assets/.gitkeep (0 bytes)
- Installing packages (npm)...
 packages (npm)...
- Installing packages (npm)...

√ Packages installed successfully.

C:\Users\Hp\Desktop\Angular>
```

Here I created project file as name CRUD-Chapter12

Also we are going to install two pacakges i.e bootstrap and angularfire in our project file.

- Command to add bootstrap

  -npm install boostrap

- Command to add angularfire

  -npm install firebase angularfire2 –save

After successful installation open the project folder in code editor to add or edit our project code.

app.module.ts

import { BrowserModule } from '@angular/platform-browser';
import { NgModule } from '@angular/core';
import { HttpModule } from '@angular/http';
import { AngularFireModule } from 'angularfire2';
import { AppComponent } from './app.component';
export const firebaseConfig = {
apiKey: "AIzaSyBN9WlmRc3SedmC4agM1G-rYqezGR22iZE",
authDomain: "crudproject-45834.firebaseapp.com",
databaseURL: "https://crudproject-45834.firebaseio.com",
storageBucket: "crudproject-45834.appspot.com",
messagingSenderId: "590481645308"
};
@NgModule({

```
declarations: [
AppComponent
],
imports: [
BrowserModule,
HttpModule,
AngularFireModule.initializeApp(firebaseConfig)
],
providers: [],
bootstrap: [AppComponent]
})
export class AppModule {
}
```

Code explanation:

import {AngularFireModule} from 'angularfire2';

we have imports the AngularFireModule class from the AngularFire2 library. This class is used to initialize the AngularFire2 library in an Angular application.

The AngularFire2 library provides Angular bindings for Firebase, a popular backend platform. By using AngularFire2, Angular developers can easily access Firebase features such as real-time database, authentication, and storage.

app.component.ts

```
import { Component, OnInit } from '@angular/core';
import { AngularFire} from 'angularfire2';
@Component({
selector: 'app-root',
template: `
`
})
export class AppComponent {
constructor(af: AngularFire){
console.log(af);
}
}
```

The bold line that we added in app.component.ts means that a constructor of a class in an Angular application is what you gave in the code. The 'AngularFire' service, which is offered by the 'angularfire2' library, is injected as a dependency in the constructor.

A design approach called dependency injection in Angular lets you give instances of dependencies to a class or component. It is beneficial to manage and decouple the dependencies of various application components.

12.5 Working with a Fire

A NoSQL database is a type of database that does not use the traditional relational database model. Instead, NoSQL databases store data in a more flexible way, typically using a key-value or document model.

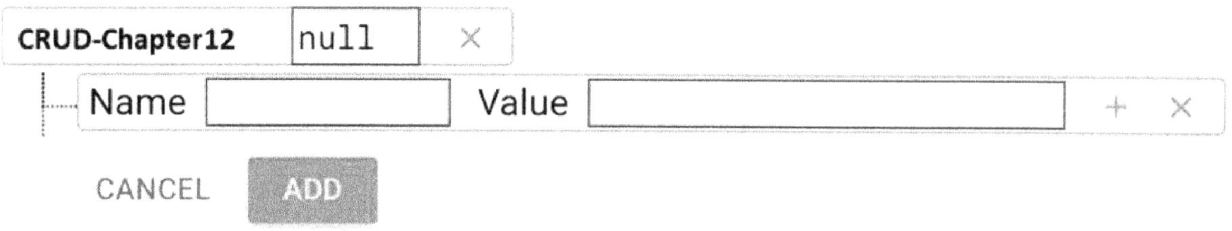

In the text, you are being shown how to use the Firebase database, which is a NoSQL database. The Firebase database is a tree of key-value pair objects. This means that data is stored in a hierarchy of nodes, where each node has a key and a value. The key is a unique identifier for the node, and the value is the data that is stored at that node.

```
students-list
  -NICiDK5QYBCjK2Kd5V9
    email: "faizanshah@gmail.com"
    firstName: "Faizan "
    lastName: "Shah"
    mobileNumber: "77047000000"
  -NICiLc61BUBeRg2VjqV
    email: "rehanshah@gmail.com"
    firstName: "Rehan "
    lastName: Shah
    mobileNumber: "9022060000"
```

You can add new nodes to the tree by clicking on the "+" button. When you add a new node, you need to specify the key and the value for that node. The key can be a string, a number, or a boolean value. The value can be any type of data, including strings, numbers, boolean values, objects, or arrays.

You can also add complex objects to the Firebase database. A complex object is an object that contains other objects. For example, you could create a complex object that contains the user's name, email address, and phone number.

The Firebase database is a powerful tool for storing data. It is flexible, scalable, and easy to use. If you are looking for a database for your next project, I recommend that you consider using the Firebase database.

Here are some additional details about the Firebase database:

- The Firebase database is a real-time database, which means that changes to data are immediately reflected to all clients that are connected to the database.
-
- The Firebase database is a cloud-based database, which means that you do not need to worry about managing the database yourself.
- The Firebase database is a free service, but there are paid plans available for businesses that need more features or capacity.

12.6 Displaying List of Users

user.component.ts

```
import { Component, OnInit } from '@angular/core';
import { AngularFire } from 'angularfire2';
@Component({
selector: 'users',
templateUrl: './user.component.html'
})
export class UserComponent {
users;
constructor(private af:AngularFire){
}
ngOnInit(){
this.users = this.af.database.list('/');
}
}
```

Code Explanation:

import { Component, OnInit } from '@angular/core';

This line imports the `Component` and `OnInit` classes from the Angular core library. The `Component` class is used to create Angular components, and the `OnInit` class is used to indicate that a component has been initialized.

import { AngularFire } from 'angularfire2';

This line imports the `AngularFire` class from the AngularFire2 library. The `AngularFire` class provides access to Firebase services, such as the database, storage, and authentication services.

```
@Component({
selector: 'users',
templateUrl: './user.component.html'
})
```

This line defines the component metadata for the `UserComponent` class. The `selector` property specifies the CSS selector that is used to select the component, and the `templateUrl` property specifies the path to the HTML template file that is used to render the component.

```
export class UserComponent {
users;
constructor(private af:AngularFire){
}
```

This line declares the `UserComponent` class. The `export` keyword makes the class available to other modules.

This line declares a public property named `users`. This property will be used to store the list of users.

This line calls the constructor for the `UserComponent` class. The `af` property is injected into the constructor by Angular. This property is an instance of the `AngularFire` class, and it will be used to access the Firebase database.

```
ngOnInit(){
this.users = this.af.database.list('/');
}
```

This line calls the `ngOnInit()` method. This method is called when the component has been initialized. In this case, the `ngOnInit()` method uses the `af.database.list()` method to get a list of users from the Firebase database. The list of users is then stored in the `users` property.

user.component.html

we are going to create user.component.html with the following code

```
<h1>Users</h1>
```

```
<table class="table table-bordered">
<thead>
<tr>
<th>Username</th>
<th>Email</th>
<th>Edit</th>
<th>Delete</th>
</tr>
</thead>
<tbody>
<tr *ngFor="let user of users | async">
<td>{{ user.name }}</td>
<td>{{ user.email }}</td>
<td>
<a>
<i class="glyphicon glyphicon-edit"></i>
</a>
</td>
<td>
<a>
<i class="glyphicon glyphicon-remove"></i>
</a>
</td>
</tr>
</tbody>
</table>
```

Code Explanation:

```
<h1>Users</h1>
```

This line creates an HTML heading element with the text "Users".

```
<table class="table table-bordered">
```

This line creates an HTML table element with the class "table table-bordered". The "table table-bordered" class will add a border around the table and make the table cells look a bit different.

```
<thead>
```

This line creates an HTML table head element. The table head element will contain the table headers.

```
<tr>
```

This line creates an HTML table row element. The table row element will contain the table cells for the table headers.

```
<th>Username</th>
<th>Email</th>
<th>Edit</th>
<th>Delete</th>
```

These lines create four HTML table cells. The first cell will contain the text "Username", the second cell will contain the text "Email", the third cell will contain the text "Edit", and the fourth cell will contain the text "Delete".

```
</tr>
</thead>
<tbody>
```

These lines close the table head element and open the table body element. The table body element will contain the table rows for the user data.

```
<tr *ngFor="let user of users | async">
```

This line creates an HTML table row element for each user in the `users` array. The `*ngFor` directive will iterate over the `users` array and create a new table row for each user. The `async` pipe will ensure that the user data is loaded asynchronously.

```
<td>{{ user.name }}</td>
<td>{{ user.email }}</td>
<td>
<a>
<i class="glyphicon glyphicon-edit"></i>
</a>
</td>
<td>
<a>
<i class="glyphicon glyphicon-remove"></i>
</a>
</td>
```

These lines create four HTML table cells for each user. The first cell will contain the user's name, the second cell will contain the user's email address, the third cell will contain a link to edit the user, and the fourth cell will contain a link to delete the user.

```
</tr>
</tbody>
</table>
```

These lines close the table body element and the table element. After create a file name as app.routing.ts as below.

app.routing.ts

```
import { RouterModule } from ‘@angular/router’;
import { UserComponent } from ‘./user.component’;
export const routing = RouterModule.forRoot([
{ path:‘', component:UserComponent },
]);
```

There is just one route that leads to the user component at the moment. Later, we will add a route to the User Add and Edit form to the existing routes.

app.module.ts

Add the bold code in app.module.ts after adding it look like as follow,

```
import { BrowserModule } from '@angular/platform-browser‘;
import { NgModule } from '@angular/core‘;
import { HttpModule } from '@angular/http‘;
import { AngularFireModule } from 'angularfire2‘;
import { AppComponent } from './app.component‘;
import { UserComponent } from './user.component‘;
import { routing } from './app.routing‘;
export const firebaseConfig = {
apiKey: "AIzaSyAxTQHg5UhuI5M_hlVqaaca4sQwUGYXdsQ",
authDomain: "crud-chapter12-4954e.firebaseapp.com",
projectId: "crud-chapter12-4954e",
storageBucket: "crud-chapter12-4954e.appspot.com",
messagingSenderId: "826189123510"};
@NgModule({
declarations: [
```

```
AppComponent,
UserComponent,
],
imports: [
BrowserModule,
HttpModule,
AngularFireModule.initializeApp(firebaseConfig),
routing
],
providers: [],
bootstrap: [AppComponent]
})
export class AppModule {
}
```

app.component.ts

```
import { Component } from '@angular/core';
@Component({
selector: 'app-root',
templateUrl: './app.component.html',
styleUrls: ['./app.component.scss']
})
export class AppComponent {
title = 'CRUD-Chapter12';
}
```

index.html

In index.html we will add bootstrap link so that our table border render correctly.

```
<!doctype html>
<html>
<head>
<meta charset="utf-8">
<title>CRUDproject</title>
<base href="/">
<meta name="viewport" content="width=device-width, initial-scale=1">
<link rel="icon" type="image/x-icon" href="favicon.ico">
<link rel="stylesheet"
href="https://maxcdn.bootstrapcdn.com/bootstrap/3.3.7/css/bootstrap.min.css" integrity="sha384-
BVYiiSIFeK1dGmJRAkycuHAHRg32OmUcww7on3RYdg4Va+PmSTsz/K68vbdEjh4u"
crossorigin="anonymous">
</head>
<body>
<app-root>Loading...</app-root>
</body>
</html>
```

12.7 Adding User

user.component.html

Adding a user to our programme will be implemented next. Before the user list in user.component.html, first create a button with the name create User. Put btn and btn-primary button classes in CSS to decorate it as seen below.

```
<h1>Users</h1>
<button class="btn btn-primary" (click)="add()">Add</button>
<table class="table table-bordered">
```

user.component.ts

A new page with a form to add a new user is directed to when we click this button. Use the add() function in user.component.ts as seen below to construct this route.

```
import { Component, OnInit } from '@angular/core';
import { AngularFire } from 'angularfire2';
import { Router } from '@angular/router';
@Component({
selector: 'users',
templateUrl: './user.component.html'
})
export class UserComponent {
users;
constructor(private af:AngularFire, private _router: Router){
}
ngOnInit(){
this.users = this.af.database.list('/');
}
add(){
this._router.navigate(['add']);
}
}
```

app.routing.ts

Import the UserForm component's path and add it as seen below in app.routing.ts. The subsequent step is where we'll develop the UserForm component.

```
import { RouterModule } from '@angular/router';
import { UserComponent } from './user.component';
import { UserFormComponent } from './user-form.component';
export const routing = RouterModule.forRoot([
{ path:'', component:UserComponent },
{ path:'add',component:UserFormComponent }
]);
```

user.ts

We represent the model data behind our User form with the class User in user.ts . So add this class in app .

```
export class User{
id: string;
username: string;
email: string;
}
```

user-form.component.ts

Create the user-form.component.ts component, which implements a model-driven form with the fields username and email, as shown below.

```
import { Component } from '@angular/core';
```

```
import { FormBuilder, FormGroup, Validators } from '@angular/forms';
import { Router } from '@angular/router';
import { AngularFire } from 'angularfire2';
import { User } from './user';
@Component({
selector:'user-form',
templateUrl: 'user-form.component.html'
})
export class UserFormComponent {
form: FormGroup;
title: string;
user = new User();
constructor(fb: FormBuilder, private _router:Router,
private af:AngularFire){
this.form = fb.group({
username:['',Validators.required ],
email:['',Validators.required]
})
}
ngOnInit(){
this.title = "New User";
}
submit(){
this.af.database.list('/').push({
name: this.user.username,
email: this.user.email
});
this._router.navigate(['']);
}
}
```

Code Explanation:

import { Component } from '@angular/core';

This line imports the `**Component**` class from the Angular core library. The `**Component**` class is used to create Angular components.

import { FormBuilder, FormGroup, Validators } from '@angular/forms';

This line imports the `**FormBuilder**`, `**FormGroup**`, and `**Validators**` classes from the Angular forms library. The `**FormBuilder**` class is used to create and manage forms, the `**FormGroup**` class is used to represent a form, and the `**Validators**` class provides a set of validation rules.

import { Router } from '@angular/router';

This line imports the `**Router**` class from the Angular router library. The `**Router**` class is used to navigate between different components in an Angular application.

import { AngularFire } from 'angularfire2';

This line imports the `**AngularFire**` class from the AngularFire2 library. The `**AngularFire**` class provides access to Firebase services, such as the database, storage, and authentication services.

import { User } from './user';

This line imports the `**User**` class from the `user` module. The `**User**` class represents a user in the application.

@Component({
selector:'user-form',

```
templateUrl: 'user-form.component.html'
})
```

This line defines the component metadata for the `UserFormComponent` class. The `selector` property specifies the CSS selector that is used to select the component, and the `templateUrl` property specifies the path to the HTML template file that is used to render the component.

```
export class UserFormComponent {
form: FormGroup;
title: string;
user = new User();
```

This line declares the `UserFormComponent` class. The `export` keyword makes the class available to other modules. The `form` property is a form that is used to collect user input. The `title` property is the title of the form. The `user` property is a new instance of the `User` class.

```
constructor(fb: FormBuilder, private _router:Router,
private af:AngularFire){
this.form = fb.group({
username:['',Validators.required ],
email:['',Validators.required]
})
}
```

This line calls the constructor for the `UserFormComponent` class. The `fb` property is injected into the constructor by Angular. This property is an instance of the `FormBuilder` class, and it will be used to create the form. The `_router` property is injected into the constructor by Angular. This property is an instance of the `Router` class, and it will be used to navigate between different components in the application. The `af` property is injected into the constructor by Angular. This property is an instance of the `AngularFire` class, and it will be used to access the Firebase database.

```
ngOnInit(){
this.title = "New User";
}
```

This line calls the `ngOnInit()` method. This method is called when the component has been initialized. In this case, the `ngOnInit()` method sets the `title` property to the text "New User".

```
submit(){
this.af.database.list('/').push({
name: this.user.username,
email: this.user.email
});
this._router.navigate(['']);
}
```

This line calls the `submit()` method. This method is called when the user submits the form. In this case, the `submit()` method uses the `af.database.list()` method to push a new user to the Firebase database. The `name` and `email` properties of the user are used to create the new user in the database. The `method is then used to navigate to the home page of the application. **_router.navigate()**`

12.8 FirebaseListObservable Push

The `submit()` method is called when the user submits the form. The form is a component that is used to collect user input. The `submit()` method uses the `af.database.list()` method to push a new user to the Firebase database. The `af.database.list()` method is a method of the `AngularFire` class. The `AngularFire` class provides access to Firebase services, such as the database, storage, and authentication services.

Here is a more detailed explanation of the `**submit()**` method:

```
submit(){
// Get the user input from the form.
const username = this.user.username;
const email = this.user.email;
// Create a new user object.
const user = {
name: username,
email: email
};
// Push the user to the Firebase database.
this.af.database.list('/').push(user);
// Navigate to the home page of the application.
this._router.navigate(['']);
}
```

Create the template name as userform component in user-form.component.html with following code

user-form.component.html

```
<h1>{{ title }}</h1>
<form [formGroup]="form" (ngSubmit)="submit()">
<div class="form-group">
<label for="username">Username</label>
<input [(ngModel)]="user.username" type="text" class="form-control"
formControlName="username">
<div *ngIf="form.controls.username.touched &&
!form.controls.username.valid" class="alert alert-danger">
Username is required
</div>
</div>
<div class="form-group">
<label for="email">Email</label>
<input [(ngModel)]="user.email" class="form-control"
formControlName="email">
<div *ngIf="form.controls.email.touched && form.controls.email.errors">
<div *ngIf="form.controls.email.errors.required"
class="alert alert-danger">
Email is required.
</div>
</div>
</div>
<button [disabled]="!form.valid" class="btn btn-primary" type="submit">{{ title }}</button>
</form>
```

Code Explanation:

The code creates a form that is used to collect user input. The form is a component that is used to collect user input. The form has two fields, a username field and an email field. The username field is required, and the email field is also required. The form is submitted when the user clicks on the "Submit" button.

```
<h1>{{ title }}</h1>
```

This line creates an HTML heading element with the text "Users".

```
<form [formGroup]="form" (ngSubmit)="submit()">
```

This line creates an HTML form element. The `**formGroup**` property is bound to the `**form**` property of the `**UserFormComponent**` class. The `**ngSubmit**` event binding is used to call the `**submit()**` method when the user submits the form.

```
<div class="form-group">
<label for="username">Username</label>
<input [(ngModel)]="user.username" type="text" class="form-control"
formControlName="username">
<div *ngIf="form.controls.username.touched &&
!form.controls.username.valid" class="alert alert-danger">
Username is required
</div>
</div>
```

This line creates an HTML form group element. The `**form-group**` class is used to style the form group. The `**label**` element is used to label the username field. The `**input**` element is used to collect the username input from the user. The `**ngModel**` directive is used to bind the `**user.username**` property to the `**input**` element. The `**formControlName**` property is used to specify the name of the form control. The `***ngIf**` directive is used to display an alert message if the username field is not filled in.

```
<div class="form-group">
<label for="email">Email</label>
<input [(ngModel)]="user.email" class="form-control"
formControlName="email">
<div *ngIf="form.controls.email.touched && form.controls.email.errors">
<div *ngIf="form.controls.email.errors.required"
class="alert alert-danger">
Email is required.
</div>
</div>
</div>
```

This line creates an HTML form group element. The `**form-group**` class is used to style the form group. The `**label**` element is used to label the email field. The `**input**` element is used to collect the email input from the user. The `**ngModel**` directive is used to bind the `**user.email**` property to the `**input**` element. The `**formControlName**` property is used to specify the name of the form control. The `***ngIf**` directive is used to display an alert message if the email field is not filled in or if the email is not in the correct format.

```
<button [disabled]="!form.valid" class="btn btn-primary" type="submit">{{ title }}</button>
</form>
```

This line creates a button that is used to submit the form. The `**disabled**` property is used to disable the button if the form is not valid. The `**class**` property is used to style the button. The `**type**` property is used to specify the type of the button. The `**ngSubmit**` event binding is used to call the `**submit()**` method when the user clicks on the button.

app.module.ts

Finally, we import ReactiveFormsModule in app.module.ts since model driven forms require it. We import the UserForm Component as well and specify that it belongs in the App Module.

```
import { BrowserModule } from '@angular/platform-browser';
import { NgModule } from '@angular/core';
import { ReactiveFormsModule } from '@angular/forms';
import { HttpModule } from '@angular/http';
import { AngularFireModule } from 'angularfire2';
import { AppComponent } from './app.component';
```

```
import { UserComponent } from './user.component';
import { UserFormComponent } from './user-form.component';
import { routing } from './app.routing';
export const firebaseConfig = {
apiKey: "AIzaSyAxTQHg5UhuI5M_hlVqaaca4sQwUGYXdsQ",
authDomain: "crud-chapter12-4954e.firebaseapp.com",
projectId: "crud-chapter12-4954e",
storageBucket: "crud-chapter12-4954e.appspot.com",
messagingSenderId: "826189123510"
};
@NgModule({
declarations: [
AppComponent,
UserComponent,
UserFormComponent,
],
imports: [
BrowserModule,
ReactiveFormsModule,
HttpModule,
AngularFireModule.initializeApp(firebaseConfig),
routing
],
providers: [],
bootstrap: [AppComponent]
})
export class AppModule {
}
```

Running App:

Start using your application right away. After filling out the Add form with your new username and email, you should be able to see your new user object added to the list.

12.9 Deleting User

When we click the delete symbol in a user's row of the user list to delete a user, a confirmation popup will question us whether we really want to do so.

user.component.html

First, in user.component.html, the delete icon's click event is bound to the delete() function, which takes a user object (from Firebase) as an argument.

```
<h1>Users</h1>
<button class="btn btn-primary" (click)="add()">Add</button>
<table class="table table-bordered">
<thead>
<tr>
<th>Username</th>
<th>Email</th>
<th>Edit</th>
<th>Delete</th>
</tr>
</thead>
<tbody>
<tr *ngFor="let user of users | async">
<td>{{ user.name }}</td>
<td>{{ user.email }}</td>
<td>
<a>
<i class="glyphicon glyphicon-edit"></i>
```

```
</a>
</td>
<td>
<a>
<i (click)="delete(user)" class="glyphicon glyphicon-remove"></i>
</a>
</td>
</tr>
</tbody>
</table>
```

user.component.ts

We implement the delete() method as shown below in user.component.ts.

```
import { Component, OnInit } from '@angular/core';
import { AngularFire } from 'angularfire2';
import { Router } from '@angular/router';
@Component({
selector: 'users',
templateUrl: './user.component.html'
})
export class UserComponent {
users;
constructor(private af:AngularFire, private _router: Router){
}
ngOnInit(){
this.users = this.af.database.list('/');
}
add(){
this._router.navigate(['add']);
}
delete(user){
if (confirm("Are you sure you want to delete " + user.name + "?")){
this.af.database.object(user.$key).remove()
.then( x=> console.log("SUCCESS"))
.catch( error => {
alert("Could not delete the user.");
console.log("ERROR", error)
});
}
}
}
```

In the remove() method, we first show a confirmation box that requests your approval before deleting anything. If so, we use this.af.database.object's delete() function.

this.af.database.object(user.$key).remove()

We may retrieve a single, specified item from Firebase using the object() function. The location of the data in Firebase must be specified as an argument in object(). In this instance, the user object that we clicked to remove has the object's location information in its $key attribute. We acquired this $key property, but how? An exclusive key is produced for us each time we upload an item to Firebase. In order to obtain the object for deletion as well as later retrieval and modification, we need the distinct key contained in $key.

Once the relevant object has been identified using object(), we execute the delete() function to remove it from Firebase. whether you want to be alerted whether the deletion is successful, you may choose to subscribe to the promise that delete() returns. (Push() and update() behave similarly.)

```
this.af.database.object(user.$key).remove()
.then( x=> console.log("SUCCESS"))
.catch( error => {
alert("Could not delete the user.");
console.log("ERROR", error)
});
```

If everything goes well, "**Success**" is recorded, and if a problem occurs, an error message is recorded.

12.10 Populating the Form on Edit

After putting into practise list, add, and delete, we will now put into practise edit. The required user object must first be retrieved and filled up on the form before we can implement edit. A user will be sent to the User Form after clicking the Edit icon, where the user data will already be filled out in the input boxes. Additionally, we switch the page's name from Add User to Edit User. And if we use the Add User button to open the User Form, the headline should read New User.

As seen below, we first establish a new route add/:id in app.routing.ts with id as a parameter. The value of id will be the user object id that was used to fill the Edit form and obtain our user object.

app.routing.ts

```
import { RouterModule } from '@angular/router';
import { UserComponent } from './user.component';
import { UserFormComponent } from './user-form.component';
export const routing = RouterModule.forRoot([
{ path:'', component:UserComponent },
{ path:'add',component:UserFormComponent },
{ path:'add/:id', component: UserFormComponent }
]);
```

user.component.html

Next, we add the router link to the Editicon in user.component.html, using the argument user.$key to get our user object and fill out our form.

```
<a [routerLink]="['/add', user.$key]">
<i class="glyphicon glyphicon-edit"></i>
</a>
```

user-form.component.ts

Add the bolded codes below to user-form.component.ts next.

```
import { Component } from '@angular/core';
import { FormBuilder, FormGroup, Validators } from '@angular/forms';
import { Router, ActivatedRoute } from '@angular/router';
import { AngularFire } from 'angularfire2';
import { User } from './user';
@Component({
selector:'user-form',
templateUrl: 'user-form.component.html'
})
export class UserFormComponent {
id;
```

```
form: FormGroup;
title: string;
user = new User();
item;
constructor(fb: FormBuilder, private _router:Router, private _route:ActivatedRoute, private
af:AngularFire){
this.form = fb.group({
username:['',Validators.required ],
email:['',Validators.required]
})
}
ngOnInit(){
this._route.params.subscribe(params => {
this.id = params["id"];
});
if(!this.id){
this.title = "New User";
}
else{
this.title = "Edit User";
this.item = this.af.database.object(this.id);
}
}
submit(){
this.af.database.list('/').push({
name: this.user.username,
email: this.user.email
});
this._router.navigate(['']);
}
```

Code Explanation:

import { Router, ActivatedRoute } from '@angular/router';

We inject ActivatedRoute into our constructor after importing it. As seen below, this is utilised to obtain the parameter id supplied by the User component.

We grab the id from the _route.params and if it's null, we know we've reached the UserForm without a parameter and want to add a new user. Thus, we changed the title to "New User."

```
ngOnInit(){
this._route.params.subscribe(params => {
this.id = params["id"];
});
if(!this.id){
this.title = "New User";
}
else{
this.title = "Edit User";
this.item = this.af.database.object(this.id);
}
}
```

If id is not null, it signifies we wish to edit the user with that particular id, then the headline will be displayed as "Edit User". Then we carry out the following code to obtain the user object:

this.item = this.af.database.object(this.id);

We utilise the object method to retrieve our user object, which we then add to the item variable. We can fill up our edit form now that item contains the user object we required.

user-form.component.html

The two bolded sections of code below should be added to user-form.component.html.

```
<h1>{{ title }}</h1>
<form [formGroup]="form" (ngSubmit)="submit()">
<div class="form-group">
<label for="username">Username</label>
<input [(ngModel)]="user.username" type="text" class="form-control"
formControlName="username" value={{(item|async)?.name}}>
<div *ngIf="form.controls.username.touched &&
!form.controls.username.valid" class="alert alert-danger">
Username is required
</div>
</div>
<div class="form-group">
<label for="email">Email</label>
<input [(ngModel)]="user.email" class="form-control"
formControlName="email" value={{(item|async)?.email}}>
<div *ngIf="form.controls.email.touched && form.controls.email.errors">
<div *ngIf="form.controls.email.errors.required"
class="alert alert-danger">
Email is required.
</div>
</div>
</div>
<button [disabled]="!form.valid" class="btn btn-primary" type="submit">{{ title }}</button>
</form>
```

The value attribute of the username and email input fields are filled with data from the item object by the code above. The values are rendered using string interpolation using the function (item|async)?.email. As was already said, we utilise the async pipe to subscribe to item, a FirebaseObjectObservable, in order to check for the most recent value released.

We must use the elvis operator after applying the async pipe, right? This indicates that we only have access to the email property if item|async is not null. This is due to the fact that item|async is produced dynamically at runtime and may initially be null because there is a slight delay between the time we subscribe and the time we receive the firebase result.

12.11 Updating a User

Finally, we add some new code to submit() in user-form.component.ts to update the user. Put the following code in the submit() box.

user-form.component.ts

```
submit(){
if (this.id) {
this.af.database.object(this.id).update({
```

```
name: this.user.username,
email: this.user.email
});
}
else{
this.af.database.list('/').push({
name: this.user.username,
email: this.user.email
});
}
this._router.navigate(['']);
}
```

Code Explanation:

The form is in edit mode if there is an ID, so we first check for that. In that case, we use the object's update function. If not, which indicates that the form is in Add New User mode, we run the object's push() method to add the new user object to Firebase.

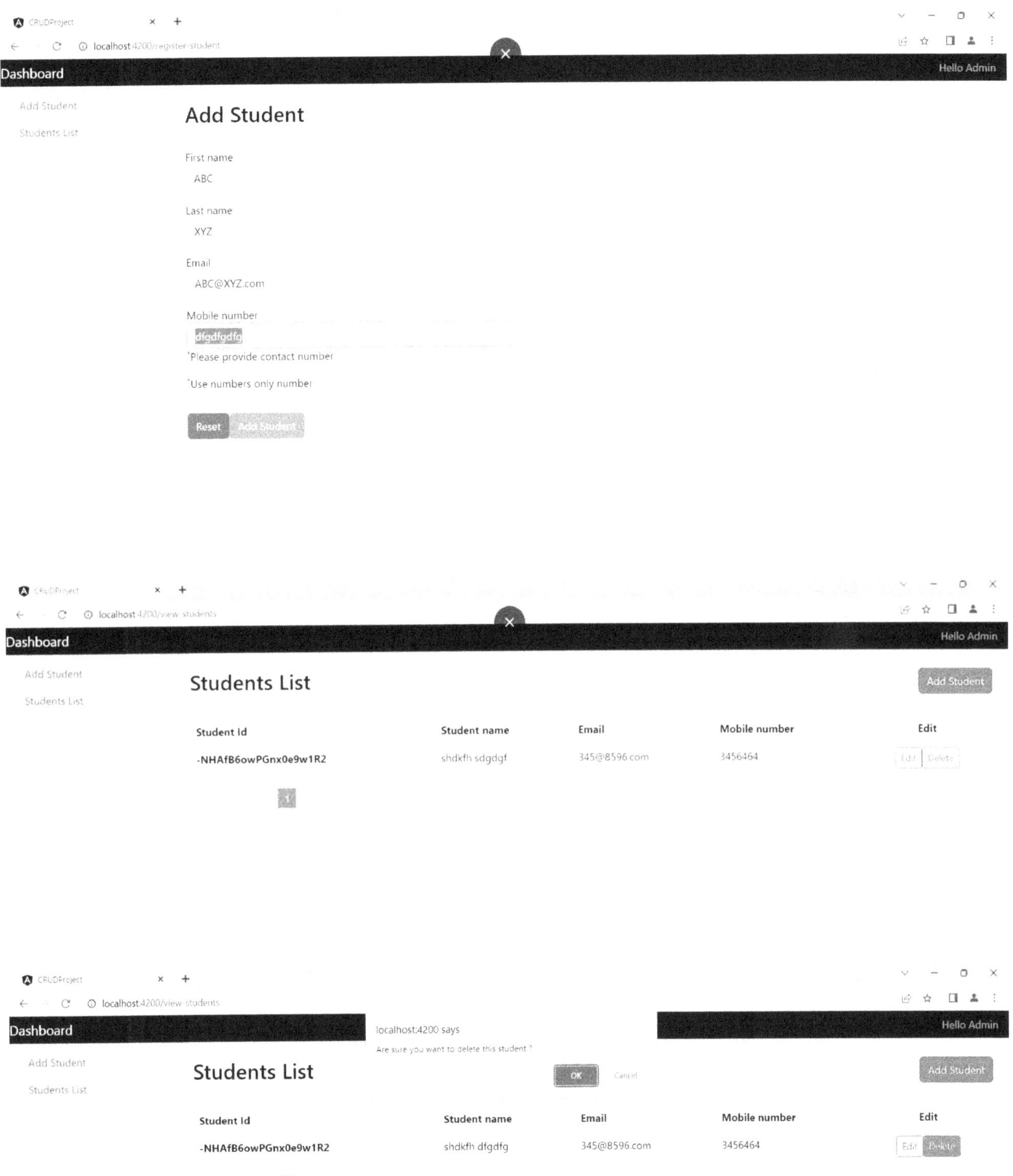
Dashboard
Hello Admin
Add Student
Students List
Add Student
First name
ABC
Last name
XYZ
Email
ABC@XYZ.com
Mobile number
dfgdfgdfg
*Please provide contact number
*Use numbers only number
Reset
Add Student
Dashboard
Hello Admin
Students List
Add Student
Student Id
Student name
Email
Mobile number
Edit
-NHAfB6owPGnx0e9w1R2
shdkfh sdgdgf
345@8596.com
3456464
localhost:4200 says
OK
Students List
Student Id
Student name
Email
Mobile number
Edit
-NHAfB6owPGnx0e9w1R2
shdkfh dfgdfg
345@8596.com
3456464

www.ingramcontent.com/pod-product-compliance
Ingram Content Group UK Ltd.
Pitfield, Milton Keynes, MK11 3LW, UK
UKHW062008290726
14090UKWH00022B/1449

9 798891 866980